Communicating Beyond our Differences...

Introducing the Psycho-Geometrics™ System

Susan Dellinger, Ph.D

JADE INK
5701 Mariner #601
Tampa, FL 33609

Publishing History: 1989 by   Prentice-Hall, Inc.
Englewood Cliffs, NJ
1996 by   Jade Ink
Tampa, FL

International Distribution: Australia, Brazil, Canada
India, Mexico, Tokyo, Russia,
Singapore, United Kingdom.

JADE INK
5701 Mariner #601
Tampa, FL 33609

Ordering/Shipping Information: 1-800-762-3478

ISBN 1-892762-00-5

51495>

9 781892 762009

Acknowledgments. . . .

To Bob (the squiggle): For the brilliance of the idea of the "shapes in evolution."

To Jade (the triangle): For the willingness to share his mind, love, and word processor.

To Haloli (the circle): For providing a Piscean balance to this driving Capricorn.

To Prentice Hall (the boxes): For performing their editorial duties with methodical perfection and true caring.

To all of my Seminar Participants: For thoroughly enjoying Psycho-Geometrics and encouraging me to finally write this book.

Introduction

How Psycho-Geometrics Can Help You

You are about to receive a gift! The gift of knowledge that will help you (1) to know yourself better and (2) to understand other people in your life (both professional and personal). The greatest thing about this new system is that it's so *simple* . . . . and it *works*!

As these pages unfold before you, you will experience the "newest" form of personality analysis . . . . the Psycho-Geometrics system. This is a unique way of looking at how and why people are different. We are all different, one from another. This is one of the true joys of living! Wouldn't it be boring if we were all the same?

You might agree with me that it would be boring, but you might also say it would be a lot easier to *communicate* if people saw the world in the same way.

"Why *does* that 'jerk' act that way at work?"

"How can your spouse be so insensitive?"

And, of course,

"What's the matter with kids tooo . . . . day?"

By learning Psycho-Geometrics, you will be able to answer these questions; you will be able to explain why the important people in your life behave as they do. This will improve and enhance all of your relationships. *That is a gift!*

BENEFITS OF THE BOOK

1. You will understand why you are attracted to certain people, and not to others.

2. You will understand why certain people "put you off," and why you seem to have *good chemistry* almost instantly with some people you meet.

3. You will learn why you have difficulty communicating with certain individuals—both at work and in your social life.

4. It will become clear to you that those people see the world (and even the same situation) differently than you do.

5. You will learn *why* people have differing perceptions based on their upbringing, their personality, and the unique way in which their brains function.

6. Your boss, spouse, co-workers, and kids will suddenly become *open books* to you!

7. And . . . . because of this, your communication with them will improve *overnight*! You will suddenly be able to perceive the world as *they* see it.

8. In addition to improving your communication with others, this book will give you increased *self-knowledge*. You will learn why *you* think and behave as you do.

9. All of these benefits will result in increased *self-confidence* for you. You will find yourself with a new "lease on life" because you are now prepared to deal with those *difficult people*. And you will have new love and appreciation for those "significant others" in your personal life.

10. Finally, you will find invigorating *motivation* to go right out and apply the psycho-geometric method! You will begin to "see" people according to their geometric personality; and when you do, you will find out that it works . . . . immediately!

HOW TO READ THE BOOK

Chapter One, "Play the Game," introduces you to the method. In it, you will analyze yourself and understand why you behave as you do. If you are like most people who first learn the method, you will stop reading after Chapter One and run out and try the method on the closest person you can find! You will receive the gift immediately! (Note: This is not a heavily *academic* and *intellectual* method that you must study for years to understand. It's quick, simple, and immediately useful.

Next, you will want to read more, and more about it! Sections One,

Two, Three, Four, and Five will thoroughly "clue you in" on each one of the five personality types. Section One describes the *Box* person, Section Two the *Triangle* person, Section Three describes the *Rectangle* person, Section Four is devoted to the *Circle* person, and Section Five describes the *Squiggle*. Each Section consists of four chapters devoted to each type. You may want to skip over to your type immediately and return to read about the other four types later.

Section Six is called Shape Flexing. This is a very important section because, in it, you will learn how to adjust your style of communication to the style of others . . . . we call this flexing. In order for the method to be most useful to you in your everyday life, you must learn to *flex to others*. Chapter Twenty-Two will teach you to Flex with Finesse.

Chapter Twenty-Three gives you a greater understanding of why people change as they get older. It seems that the things that were *so* important to us when we were young just don't carry the same significance as we age. There is a way of explaining this change; it is called life stages. As we pass through predictable life stages (adolescence, young married, mid-life crisis, etc.) we are merely doing long-term flexing. Understanding these stages through the Psycho-Geometrics method makes it easier to help others, and one's self, to go through it.

The final section of the book is the Appendix. This is provided for those of you who are curious about the development and history of this method. Also, for you astrology buffs, you will find a complete charting of horoscope signs connected with the geometric types in this Appendix.

HOW PSYCHO-GEOMETRICS CAME ABOUT

I have presented the geometric analysis method to over 100,000 people in the last 12 years. As a management trainer in a major corporation (*Fortune* 25), I began using this method as an "ice-breaker" in management training programs for supervisors and middle managers. Other trainers have used it also, and today (in the training business) it is considered to be public domain.

In my training programs, I noticed that the participants became *very interested* in this little ice-breaker game. They found it to be a useful way to understand both themselves and their bosses and subordinates. So . . . . on their behalf, I began researching it. Where did it come from? Why was it such an instant hit with people?

The result of my research was ziltch! So . . . . I began to develop my own theory about how geometric shapes are significant indicators of how people think and behave. I found lots of interesting support in the classic personality theories of Dr. Carl Jung. Although the Myers-Briggs instrument was available, it was long and complicated to interpret. This method was quicker and as accurate. I changed the original training "game" to include a fifth shape, and named the method Psycho-Geometrics.

Next, I got my "act together" and took it "on the road"! In the last five years, I have presented this method as an integral part of my public seminar "Power Communication Skills," which I present throughout the nation via CareerTrack, Inc. of Boulder, Colorado. On the public circuit, I have presented this method in 25 states and overseas. *At every seminar,* participants have come up to the podium to ask, "Where can I learn more about Psycho-Geometrics?" Unfortunately, I could not recommend a source! Thus, I am writing this book and, for the first time, consolidating the numerous sources contributive to the method.

WHAT OTHERS SAY ABOUT PSYCHO-GEOMETRICS

"It has changed my life!". . . . corporate supervisor

"Why didn't I know about this 20 years ago?". . . . nurse

"Wait 'til I get to the courtroom! What a great way to evaluate potential members of the jury!". . . . lawyer

"This should be required information in our schools! It is an important 'skill for living' for our children to possess. (Not bad for teachers either.)". . . . university professor

"Finally. . . . I understand my daughter! Thank you!". . . . accountant

"Psycho-Geometrics would be an excellent method to use in placement testing for our new employees.". . . . *Fortune* 500 personnel officer

"I'm a Triangle and my new boyfriend is a Triangle too. I'm calling (long distance from California to Florida) to find out, is there any chance for us?". . . . secretary

"Thank you so much for the 'gift' of Psycho-Geometrics. I will be able to go to work tomorrow morning with confidence for the first time. I didn't understand my boss until now. Now, I'm ready for him!". . . . supervisor

"So that's what the terrible twos really means!". . . . thirtysomething mother

"Psycho-Geometrics is great at cocktail parties! I wrote it on a napkin and asked people to choose their shape. They loved it. It was the hit of the night!" . . . . real estate agent

"It's not THAT great!". . . . author's husband.

Oh yes, it is! How do I know? Because my mail and phone bills attest to it! Psycho-Geometrics has become an invaluable tool to thousands of people in this nation. Now, it can be valuable to you also! You will return to this book again and again. *Read and enjoy*!!

WHO ARE YOU?

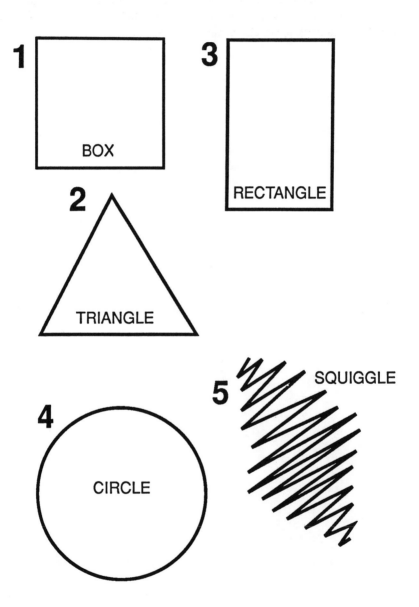

Contents

Office
Personal Habits
Body Language

Section Six *SHAPE FLEXING*

Chapter 1

Play the Game

The "game" is Psycho-Geometrics. By playing, you will learn more about yourself and the other people with whom you interact on a daily basis. The *rules of the game* are simple:

Rules: Look at the five shapes on the preceding page. Choose the shape you feel is YOU! (If you are having difficulty, choose the shape that you were first attracted to when you looked at the page.) Write the name of your preferred shape in slot #1 below. Next, rank the remaining four shapes in order of preference to you. Put the least descriptive shape in slot #5, etc.

Rank Order of Shapes

1. _____   4. _____
2. _____   5. _____
3. _____

It is important that you *write down* your order of preference, so that later you will be clear about which shapes were most descriptive of you, and which were not.

Explanation

Whichever shape you placed in the #1 slot is your *primary* shape. The significance of this shape should define your primary characteristics and why you behave as you do in this world. The next section will explain the concept of Psycho-Geometrics to you. After having read this section, you will want to jump to whichever section in the book explains your primary shape in detail. They are presented in the order that the shapes are numbered, but, it is important that you *first read* the explanation of the theory.

PSYCHO-GEOMETRICS: AN OVERVIEW

Psycho-Geometrics is based on the notion that we tend to be attracted to certain shapes and forms in our environment based on our personalities, our attitudes, our education and experiences, and based on the way in which our individual brains function.

Let's begin with *brain function*. Some people tend to access information through the left side (hemisphere) of the brain, others through the right side. How you process information in your "computer" brain determines how you will respond to the world.

Now, what was your primary shape? If you chose shape #1 (box), or shape #2 (triangle), or shape #3 (rectangle), you chose one of the *linear shapes*. People who choose the linear shapes tend to be *left-brain thinkers*. This means that they are logical and organized in their approach to life.

If you chose one of the two remaining shapes—#4 (circle) or #5 (squiggle)—you are categorized as a *right-brain thinker*. Right-brainers tend to process information they receive in a less linear and more configural (mosaic) way. They are more interested in the whole than the individual parts. Right-brainers place less emphasis on logic and organization, and tend to be more creative and intuitive.

The hemisphere of the brain that is *dominant* for you dictates how you think. For example, left-brainers process information in *sequential* format: a,b,c,d,e . . . . etc. Right-brainers' minds jump a . . . . f! It is often difficult for the two to communicate, because they do not think in the same way.

For example, a stereotypical left-brainer might be a certified public accountant (CPA). If you are a right-brainer, you may have difficulty following the myriad of rules and regulations that your CPA insists upon. On the other hand, your CPA may gasp when you walk into his/her office with your shoe box full of receipts. This type of disorganization and lack of attention to detail is anathema to a left-brain thinker.

It is very important to understand this unique difference at the very beginning, because this difference will affect the way you perceive the world around you. It will affect the way you think, act, and the people you choose to be your friends and associates. *Brain theory* is the foundation of Psycho-Geometrics.

This will all become clearer as you read the sections devoted to each of the shapes. The next few pages will give you a quick overview of each of the four shapes and their primary attributes.

BOX CHARACTERISTICS (#1)

If your primary shape (#1 on your list) was the first shape (the box figure), you are a hard worker. The most dominant characteristic of boxes is their determination to *get the job done*. When people need a task accomplished, they turn to you to get it done. And, no matter what is involved or how long it takes, once you are committed to it, you *will* persevere to the bitter end!

The reason the box is categorized as a hard worker is because the box is a geometric square—composed of equal lines and angles. For this reason, the box tends to be the most *structured* of the five shapes. Boxes place great emphasis on organization and logical structure. They need life to be predictable: everything in the *right* place at the *right* time.

Boxes are constantly organizing the people and things around them. They truly believe in the saying, "A messy desk equals a disorganized mind." Boxes make excellent *administrators*; not managers—administrators.

Boxes are strong administrators because of their almost compulsive attention to detail. The box is a data-collector. He/she loves to collect information, enter it into the database, or file it under the appropriate heading so that it is properly organized.

Of course, with every set of strengths, there are a few weaknesses also. The box is better at *following* a plan than he/she is at designing the plan. This person is a better administrator than a manager, because he/she is not a strong decision-maker. When push comes to shove, the box **procrastinates** over making a major decision. Particularly if the decision involves some "risk," the box prefers to maintain the **status quo.**

The box says; "Tell me what the rules are, tell me what the deadlines are, give me the tools to do it, and I'll get the job done for you!" But . . . . do not put the box in an amorphous situation in which the "right hand doesn't know what the left hand is doing." Boxes do not function well in situations that are ill-defined or in a constant state of flux. However, where instructions and requirements are clear, the box excels above all the other shapes!

Box Traits

Positive	Negative
organized	meticulous
detail-oriented	nit-picking
knowledgeable	procrastinating
analytical	cool, aloof

Positive	*Negative*
persevering	resistant to change
perfectionist	loner
patient	complaining

Typical Box Jobs

accountant	government worker
administrator	manual laborer
secretary	truck driver
administrative assistant	paper processor (by any title)
doctor (specialist)	bank teller
teacher	author/editor
computer programmer	

In order to gain more precise information about the box, it is necessary for you to read Section One: "The Stubborn Box." This section will give you full details (boxes love details) about how boxes behave in both social and professional situations. It will tell you how to identify a box by his/her personality, body language, and words. You will learn how to resolve conflicts and communicate more effectively with boxes in your life. Or, if you are a box, this section will point out methods you might use to improve relationships and gain increased respect from others for the excellent contribution you make to the world.

TRIANGLE CHARACTERISTICS (#2)

You triangle people are a different sort from the box, your linear cousin. Although you share the left-brain orientation of the box, you are less interested in the work itself and more interested in your *career*. As the shape indicates, the triangle is *ambitious* and his/her focus is *at the top*. Of the five shapes, the **triangle** represents **leadership.**

The triangle has symbolized leadership for centuries, probably since the time the Egyptians buried their pharaohs in pyramids. The pyramid teaches us the value of focusing our energy on the important goal. This is the singular most valuable trait of the triangle, the ability to *focus* on the goal of the moment.

Of course, the triangle always knows what the goal is because, unlike the box, the triangle is a very *decisive* person. You triangles love to make decisions—for yourselves, and for everyone else, if possible. The triangle is a very "right" person and needs to be seen by others as a smart leader. And . . . . they are usually successful. Because of their left-brain orientation, they analyze the situation swiftly and make smart decisions. Others who are less sure, are impressed and follow them without hesitation.

However, it should be mentioned that whatever decision the triangle makes, there will be something "in it" for him/her—even if it is only increased esteem from the followers. Triangles are also the best *political maneuverers* of the five shapes. They tend to reach the top of the political **hierarchy** first and may step on others to get there. Associates respect and fear them, often with no love lost.

Triangle Traits

Positive	*Negative*
leader	self-centered
focused	overloaded
decisive	dogmatic
ambitious	status oriented
competitive	political
bottom-line oriented	impatient
athletic	driven

Typical Triangle Jobs

executive	entrepreneur
manager/supervisor	politician
(depending on career stage)	business owner
hospital administrator	military officer
school administrator	orchestra conductor
law firm partner	pilot
union organizer/officer	

Remember, you triangles are fast learners and ambitious. That's why you bought this book, wasn't it? You will want to read Section 2 about triangles. This will equip you even more to move onward and (more importantly) upward. You will learn *how to persuade* people who think differently than do you and how to avoid being maneuvered into a corner by those who would appeal to your ego. This book will become one of your most treasured guides, and you will return to it many times in the future to discover how to deal with your latest "opponent."

RECTANGLE CHARACTERISTICS (#3)

If you chose the **rectangle** as your first-choice shape, you already know that you are undergoing some major *changes* within yourself! You may have just experienced a career change, or are anticipating it. You may have recently undergone a change in your personal life. The rectangle symbolizes change and a person in a state of **transition.** While the other four shapes are relatively constant predictors of human behavior, the rectangle typifies someone who is in an "unfrozen state." This is someone who is *dissatisfied* with the way life is now and is searching for a better situation.

I call the rectangular person **confused.** This is not meant in a derogatory manner. You are not less capable than the others, you are merely *unsure* of yourself at this moment in time. Please note, this is a "transitional period": you will pass through it, but it may be a rocky road for awhile.

There is a geometric reason for all of this, of course. The rectangle is not a "pure" shape of its own. It is an outgrowth and adaptation of a pure shape—the **square** (box). *Psychologically, the rectangle is a person growing out of "box" behavior.* Rectangles are often people who have been in box jobs/lives for years, and they have become bored or resentful. They have been **hard workers** for a long time, and they don't feel they have received the appropriate recognition for all their hard work.

So, plainly stated, rectangles are "sick of it!" They are tired of doing all the work and getting little or none of the credit. Their only reward seems to be *more* hard work to do! This situation can apply to housewives as well as corporate managers. Rectangles are people in a period of change. They are not quite sure where this change will take them, but they are disgruntled with the present situation and willing to try anything!

One striking characteristic of rectangles is their *unpredictability*. If you are a rectangle, you may experience changes on a daily basis. In fact, you may appear to others to be a "different person" from day to day—even within the same day! This makes others wary of you, and many may even consciously avoid you during this change period. This is only because they don't quite know how to take you. They are confused by your mercurial changes in behavior. They are trying to understand and don't want to appear stupid, thinking you must know what you're doing. Little do they know, you don't understand it either!

The good news is, rectangularism is a *stage*. Thus, it will pass! There are some very pleasant effects during this period. Rectangles are experiencing a state of *growth*, a movement to a new plateau. They feel much excitement during this period: they are *searching* and *growing* and *learning*; open to new ideas, people, and ways of thinking. It is a perfect time for you, the rectangle, to learn about Psycho-Geometrics!

Rectangle Traits

Positive	*Negative*
state of transition	confused
exciting	low self-esteem
searching	inconsistent
inquisitive	gullible
growing	ingenuine
courageous	unpredictable

Typical Rectangle Jobs/Periods

new bosses

entry-level employees/job applicants

fresh college/high school graduates

newly promoted/demoted employees

people in mid-life crisis (see Chapter 13)

adolescents

entrepreneurs

performers (stage/film/musicians)

new retirees

As a rectangle, you will want to read Section 3. You will learn more than any of the other four shapes simply because your shape is the most open to new ideas and influences. Your challenge will be to put the ideas into practice and allow them to assist you through this awkward (but exciting) period of change.

CIRCLE CHARACTERISTICS (#4)

What would we all do without your circles? You are the **lover** among us! You really, genuinely *care* about others . . . . about *people*. You will do whatever it takes to make your family, friends, and co-workers happy. Your focus is to *smooth the waters* and keep the peace.

Geometrically, the circle is the mythological symbol for **harmony**. The person who chooses it is most interested in good interpersonal relations. He/she is the "glue" that holds together the family and the work team. This is the most *sensitive* person—the one who really, genuinely *cares* about feelings.

Circles are the best **communicators** of all five shapes. This is because they are the best *listeners*, they tend to establish empathy with others quickly, and they "read" people well. A circle can tell a phony in a minute. Circles are great *team players*, very popular with work associates. However, they are often *weak business managers*.

As leaders, circles try too hard to please everyone. They attempt to keep peace and, in doing so, sometimes avoid taking the "hard line" and making the unpopular decision that may be necessary. Also, circles are often taken advantage of by stronger, more dominant personalities like *triangles*. Circles will give in to the wishes of others in order to please them. Although this is often a positive quality, it may lead others to easily wield control over them. Fortunately, circles don't seem to care who has the control.

The circle's right-brain influence stresses *integration* rather than separation. Circles are **wholistic** thinkers, interested in how everything fits together. This interest is applied primarily to all living creatures. Thus, circles are often nature lovers, adore their pets, and have large circles of friends. Circles are excellent "people" problem-solvers.

Circle's demonstrate their "harmonizing" personality on a daily basis. They are the ones who say, "Have a nice day!" It must have been a circle who invented the "smiley face" on company memos. Circles wilt in solitary jobs, they must be out working with people.

Circle Traits

Positive	Negative
friendly	overpersonal
nurturing	melancholy
persuasive	manipulative
empathic	gossipy
generous	self-blaming
stabilizing	apolitical
reflective	indecisive
	lazy

Typical Circle Jobs

secretary	counselor/mental health
nurse/doctor	professional
teacher/trainer	housewives
professor/consultant	human resources specialist
salesperson	personnel analyst

Typical Circle Jobs (*cont.*)

waitress/clerk	nuns
historians	boy/girl scout leaders
astrologers	camp counselors

There is much for you, as a circle, to learn in this book. Section 4 is devoted to information on the behavior of circles. Since circles are a right-brain shape, the *emotions* play a central part in regulating the circle's behavior. Section 4 will instruct you as to why you behave as you do and how to modify your behavior to become a more assertive and successful person in your chosen field.

SQUIGGLE CHARACTERISTICS (#5)

You "squiggles" know who you are . . . . you are *sex-crazed!* Kidding aside, this shape is symbolic of a male sperm and, surprisingly enough, people who choose it are often considered by others to be sexually attractive. However, there is a second meaning for the shape that accurately defines its dominant characteristic: *creativity*. (You may want to combine both meanings and see what you come up with!)

The squiggle symbolizes creativity because (1) it is the most unique of the five shapes, and (2) because it is the only shape that is *open-ended*, it has no closure common to the others. Thus, this shape is representative of truly *right-brain* people. You right-brainers do think differently than the rest of us. You don't use linear processes. You are more "configural" in your information processing system.

Configural thinking means that you tend to experience cognitive leaps in thinking; you *jump* to a conclusion without experiencing the more common sequential, deductive process. The linear shapes think in an a,b,c,d,e fashion. Not the squiggle. The squiggle's mind jumps directly from a to f! For this reason it is often difficult for linear thinkers to work with squiggles in a problem-solving environment. They do not perceive the world in the same way!

This is unfortunate because the truly great *ideas* in this society have been produced by squiggles! Squiggly people are always looking for *new ways* of doing it. They challenge the status quo—never happy with the ways things are and have been done in the past. Squiggles go to sleep in history class. But . . . . they are totally alert in literature class when discussing a science fiction novel. Squiggles are *future-oriented* and more interested in possibilities than reality. Thus, the others often view them as "ivory-tower" or a little "weird."

In terms of daily behavior and personality, the squiggle is the most **excitable** person of the five. When it's a new and interesting idea, the squiggle bounces off the walls telling everyone about it. The squiggle is not interested in specific details such as facts and figures; he/she uses this information to jump to an innovative idea. The squiggle disdains highly structured and mechanized work environments. He/she wants lots of *variety* and *stimulation* in the workplace. The squiggle is bored with rules and policy manuals and much more interested in the *concepts* involved. This person is intrigued with the whole rather than the parts because he/she is an *integrative* thinker. This makes it difficult for squiggles to work in highly structured situations. He/she prefers a free-flowing, creative, *independent* work situation.

When the squiggle finds this type of job, he/she comes alive, constantly thinking up new schemes and motivating everyone around him/her. The squiggle is a great "start-up" person and is most comfortable in companies and institutions where there is constant change rather than compliance with systematized procedures. Maintenance and follow-up are not his/her strong points.

Squiggle Traits

Positive	Negative
creative	disorganized
conceptual	impractical
futuristic	unrealistic
intuitive	illogical
expressive	uninhibited
motivating	evangelistic
witty	eccentric
sensuous	naïve

Typical Squiggle Jobs

strategic planner	astrologist
artist/performer/poet	inventor/chef
musician	evangelical minister/preacher
university professor/theorist	new product specialist
scientist/researcher	international sales/marketeer
artificial intelligence expert	promoter/PR director

Typical Squiggle Jobs (*cont.*)

entrepreneur   interior decorator

real estate agent

If you chose the **squiggle,** you will want to move hastily to Section 5. This reading will equip you to understand why you behave as you do and why co-workers and friends sometimes distrust you. Although others undoubtedly like you a great deal, your erratic mood shifts and changing interests often make it difficult for them to **depend** upon you to carry through on your commitments. Section 5 will assist you in understanding how to communicate more successfully with many of the linear, left-brainers in your life. This is important because linears do *outnumber* squiggles and are often in charge of the companies in which squiggles work.

★　★　★　★

Please Note: Sometimes people finish reading about their dominant shape and decide this is *not* the right one; it is not descriptive of who they really are. (This happens in approximately 15 percent of readers.) If you are one of these people, there are two reasons why you chose the "wrong" shape.

1. You chose a shape that is *not* dominant for you today, but is the type of person you are in the process of **becoming.** You have already been another shape for awhile, and chose the *new* shape that you **want to be** rather than the one you are now.

2. Or . . . . you placed a certain shape in the #1 slot today that is atypical of you because of something that has just happened in your life which has thrown you out of kilter. You are currently in an unusual state of mind that is a result of some stressful or difficult situation. In other words, you were not "yourself" when you ranked the shapes in the beginning. If this is true, merely choose the shape now that *best describes you* and continue to read the information that applies directly to your most normal *you.*

Remember, *all five shapes are within each of us!* So, we are capable of flexing the dominance from one to another as life circumstances require. You may be more prone to "shape flexing" than others. To read more about this, refer to Section Six.

★　★　★　★

SUMMARY

Boxes are hard workers, triangles are leaders, rectangles are in transition, circles are harmonizers, and squiggles are creative. Regardless of which of the five shapes you chose, you will learn things about yourself that will be *self-empowering* in communicating and working with others. Remember, there is no one "ideal" shape! Each has its special strengths and areas for improvement.

Once you have thoroughly "digested" the characteristics of your own dominant shape, you will want to use this book in a second, very important way. You will want to refer back to the shape you placed dead last in the original ordering of the five shapes. This is your **problem shape.** People who are this shape are the ones you tend to have conflicts with.

So, your next step—after reading the four chapters in the section on your dominant shape—will be to *read about the shapes that cause you problems.* By understanding them better, you will be further *empowered to communicate* more effectively with people unlike yourself. This is the true gift of Psycho-Geometrics.

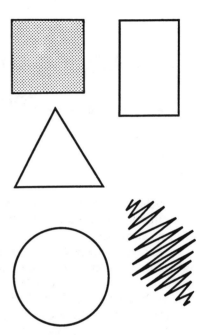

Section One

THE STUBBORN BOX

Chapter 2

Identifying the Box . . . . Find
_____ the Hardest Worker

Belief: I need to live in a **predictable world** to feel in control.

Translation: I want everything in the right place at the right time with **no surprises.**

Because boxes prefer **precise data,** I will attempt to present the information of this section in box-like language. This chapter will explain the most common beliefs and resulting behaviors associated with the box personality. We will begin with the *Quick Indications* of the box, then we will concentrate on understanding the behavior of the box at home, at work, and under stress. Each of the following four sections will have the same format for each shape.

Note: Although all of the box descriptions may *not* apply to you, *if the majority does*, then the box was the correct choice for you.

OVERVIEW

With the true box personality, the emphasis on **organization** is like a religion. It applies to all arenas of his/her life: work, home, and recreational activities. "Clean desk. . . . organized mind." The box believes that the outer environment reflects the inner self. This person is **meticulous** in his/her attention to the smallest detail. Because of the inherently strong attention to detail, the box becomes a highly **knowledgeable** person. The left-brain orientation allows the box to collect and mentally file the minutest details. Of course, boxes prefer *factual data* to information clouded with emotion or abstraction. This is also the reason that the box is very **analytical** in his/her approach

14

to life. Boxes will analyze it to death—several times before they are confident that it is the right decision. Because it takes them so long to decide, they are seen as **procrastinators** by others who make decisions more swiftly.

Boxes are often perceived by others as **cool, aloof,** and **unapproachable.** This is because they are compulsively **logical** and **practical.** They tend to be **traditionalists** in their values and beliefs. They believe strongly in the "work ethic": if one works hard and does a good job, one will be rewarded.

And work hard the box does! Boxes are the most dependable workers of all. If the box makes a commitment, you can count on it! Two of the most positive box traits are **perseverence** and **patience.** Whatever it takes to complete the task, the box will do it. However, once committed to a line of action, they become highly resistant to change. Because the box also has a strong tendency toward **perfectionism,** he/she is often perceived as a **loner** and not likely to be a team player.

QUICK INDICATORS OF BOX PEOPLE

Language

Common words: analysis, logistics, organize, allocate, assign, monitor, deadline, project, plan, database, efficiency, right, accurate

Common sayings: "The policy clearly states . . ."

"We've always done it this way."

"That's not my problem/job."

"Send it back to committee."

"Your 150-page report was bad."

"If you want a job done right, do it yourself!"

Appearance

Men: Conservative. Wouldn't dream of wearing a pastel tie (like the guys in sales do). Prefers dark suits and white shirts. Must have a handkerchief in the pocket and $10 in "mad money" in the wallet—"just in case." Hair short and no facial hair; wouldn't remotely consider a dye job or toupee. Carries comb in side pocket and a lint brush in the right hand desk drawer. Shines shoes every Sunday night. Purchases clothes at local men's shop, goes alone, and insists upon being helped by same salesman he has used in the past.

Women: Conservative also. Eschews the "latest fad." Tends to shop at medium-priced department stores and to purchase full outfits for one complete season at one time. Sticks with conservative colors of navy, brown, gray, burgundy, and black and has little variety in wardrobe. If working, clothes reflect emphasis on work, no nail polish and short cropped plain hairstyle. At home, wears plain dark slacks with sweater or t-shirt. Shoes reflect comfort as opposed to style. Box women are *never flamboyant*; a bright colored scarf at most is used. In younger days, an occasional plunging neckline or short skirt appeared, but past thirty, the "sex kitten" look becomes abhorrent to the box woman.

Office

Every pencil is in place, you bet! The desk is a sturdy wood with policy manuals lined up on the shelf above. No disorganized papers cover the desktop. The desk mat is the company-issued green felt with the matching green plastic in/out baskets and memo pad. The room is adorned with a simple photo of the family from Christmas two years ago, in a plastic frame. The walls are decorated with plaques and awards for company service and civic contributions. The college diploma (Bachelors) hangs above the umbrella stand and the box lunch is in the drawer. The focal point of the room is the large personal computer on the work table. The shelf above holds alphabetized software dating back to the advent of the computer age. *Overall impression*: A stark, sterile, functional work environment.

Personal Habits

1. **Routines.** Boxes love them. This is one of the major ways they make their worlds predictable. The box personality goes to bed at 11 P.M. and awakens at 6:30 A.M., like clockwork, every day—even Sunday. The box awakens to a well-planned day. That includes weekends. If you are a box, you do not like interruptions and unexpected callers. Boxes are heavy attendees of time management programs. Although they need it the least, they are always willing to learn more about it.

2. **Put it in writing.** The box likes tangible things. Thoughts are too evasive when expressed orally. The box needs to "see it" in print to believe. Oh . . . . and remember to cross all your t's, and be sure your margins are straight. This attention to detail is one of the hallmarks of the box personality. This applies to everything from major proposals to daily "to-do" lists. If it's recorded, it's real.

Note: I have often noticed that companies with a large paper flow are dominated by boxes. We must write memos and "c.c." everyone in the company. In fact, we write memos about the memos we already wrote. We must be sure to CYA (Cover Your Assignment)!

3. **Promptness.** You had better be on time if you have an appointment with a box! What do you think all those "to-do" lists are for? That's only a small part. Boxes keep calendars in front of them wherever they are,

fearful that they'll be late and horrified that they'll miss a commitment altogether! There are three calendars in the office (one on the desk pad, one on the wall, and a third datebook, just in case). Of course, the date book is carried on the box's body at all times and the calendar at home is updated from it every night before dinner. There is yet another calendar at home: the social calendar, but that's the least important, of course. If, perchance, the box does arrive late, it was the "secretary's fault," no doubt.

4. **Neatness.** "Who put my socks in the left hand drawer?" If you are a box, one reason "to kill" is when someone forgets to put one of your belongings in it's correct place. The paring knife goes on the left side of the silverware drawer, the scissors are kept on the third shelf, and Scotch tape and toilet paper are *always* refilled by the person who uses the last of it! These are the rules and everybody just better abide by them! If you are the roommate of a box and you have a tendency to leave your things lying around, you're in big trouble! The old comedy "The Odd Couple" was a perfect example of a box trying to live with a squiggle. A close cousin to this one is **cleanliness.** This is also important to the box. The box is horrified when he or she returns from lunch and finds the roommate is wearing it! The day is ruined. (Boxes don't allow foreign substances in their cars . . . . coffee, food, or cigarettes.)

5. **Planning.** Boxes don't do anything without planning it out first. Remember your last vacation? I'll bet it was all lined up months ahead— the hotels, rental cars, tours, meals, etc. And paid for too! In fact, the box makes three copies of the itinerary and gives them to key people just in case an unforeseen circumstance occurs. At work, boxes love **flow charts.** In fact they would flow chart the restroom and coffee breaks if given half a chance. They keep **checklists** on everything, and several extra copies of each. When boxes go on a diet, they are the only ones who really do weigh the portions to be sure they are exactly 2.5 ounces!

6. **Precision.** Whatever the box does, he/she does it with as much precision as possible. The carrots are cut as close to one-quarter inch thickness as possible. The night at the movies is planned with every contingency in mind . . . . slow service at the restaurant, a line at the box office, time for popcorn, etc. Work projects receive the same attention to detail. To the box, it's better to be "safe than sorry."

7. **Collector.** Since the time the box was a small child, he/she has collected things. It probably began with a stamp collection and progressed to baseball cards or Barbie doll sets. In fact, the box still has those childhood collections and is hoping to pass them on to his/her box child. The box adult often reflects this collector proclivity in *hobbies* such as woodwork, art collecting, macramé and crafts. Sometimes, he/she develops an avocation into a vocation (on the side) by selling the items in the collection to others.

Boxes are often members of collector groups such as autograph and historic plate societies.

8. **Social loner.** The box prefers reading, hobbies, collecting, and family activities to large group parties. The box prefers one-to-one communication over group communication. He/she reads professional journals and occasionally enjoys a mystery story or a good science fiction novel. When in social settings, the box drinks in moderation and is often viewed by others as a "wallflower." The box tends not to initiate social conversation and will often talk shop at company parties. It is not out of the realm of possibility for the box person to plan his/her social interaction for the evening—exactly who he/she will talk to and about what.

Body Language Cues

1. Stiffness of body posture; erect sitting position.
2. Absence of distracting mannerisms.
3. Perspires in social situations.
4. Perpendicular position of arms to torso when reading or gesturing.
5. Poker face, particularly in emotional situations.
6. Stilted or nervous laughter. An occasional "belly laugh" that sounds like it's coming from a different body.
7. Slightly high pitched voice than the usual relatively monotone.
8. Jerky body movements that appear when the box is uncomfortable with someone (probably a triangle or a circle). This could be a strange twitch or merely a slight jerk of the shoulder or hand.
9. Slow movement. The box does not race or run. His/her movement is purposeful and calculated.
10. Precise gestures. Although few, they are accurate.

Final Note: Yes . . . . box people are somewhat stiff and sometimes boring. But remember . . . . boxes get the job done! Companies and households alike could not function without boxes. It is the box in this society who earns the respect of others by the quality product that he/she produces.

Chapter 3

The Box at Home

Each of us is blessed with some box-like tendencies. We get organized, we straighten up the house, we clean out the office/car/closets. We each know how it feels to get into our "organized mood." Believe me, it takes a lot of box-like discipline to write this book! The difference between you and me versus the box is that the box is in his/her organized mood *constantly*!

Of course, even the box can occasionally let his/her guard down. For example, if the box works in a very structured well-defined job from 8 to 5, he/she may learn to relax and be a bit more unstructured at home. However, a *pure box* needs a higher than average amount of organization in both his/her professional and personal environments.

If you have the good fortune to live with one of these individuals, this chapter will be very important to you. It will help you create a more structured home environment to please your box spouse, child, or roommate (boxes *never* say "roomie"—circles do that). *Note*: If your box partner feels that the home is well-organized, then he/she can relax, open up, and begin to take life a little easier. Since boxes can become "workaholics," this is also for their own good.

THE BOX PARTNER/SPOUSE

Note: Although I include *partner* in this subtitle, it is unlikely that a box will "live in sin" (as grandmother says) for very long. This is a very *principled* person. Once a box falls in love, that's it! Be ready to get married post haste!

How to Create an Ideal Box Home

1. You had better be personally **clean** and **orderly** with your personal belongings. Boxes cannot tolerate clothes strewn about the house. Do not put your glass on the buffet table without a coaster under it! (Hire a housekeeper if you must!)

2. Establish a workable **routine**. Boxes need to know who does what, how, and when. Every member of the family needs a predetermined routine around the clock: family rises at 7 A.M. sharp; mother dresses children from prepared wardrobe and prepares cornflakes (7 – 7:45 A.M.); father drives kids to school on his way to work (7:45 – 8:15); mother picks up milk and cleaning on return from work (5:30 P.M.); father has dinner prepared for family consumption at 6:00 P.M. . . . etc. This is a very important element for boxes. They **do not like surprises.**

3. Design and stick to a **household budget**. Particularly if you both work, it is important to know whose money goes for what and why. Since boxes are highly **practical** people, it is unlikely that they will be willing to spend hard-earned dollars on frivolous things (like sculptured nails or St. Andrews golf putters). You may want to keep a secret "slush fund" to satisfy some of your more "squiggly" desires. Of course, there are no holds barred at Christmas and birthdays. The box respects traditional holidays, and although he/she may grumble, will not deny your pleasure at these times.

4. Save, save, save. The box is concerned about **security.** This is the person who checks with personnel about slight changes in the company retirement plan. More flamboyant boxes will make a few, very calculated personal investments, i.e., blue chip stock. In addition, the box will be able to tell you down to the penny what his/her investment is worth. Don't ask a box for financial advice unless you have two hours to kill. However, the information you receive will be totally accurate!

5. Cancel the interior decorator. The physical environment for the box should not be flashy, new, or dramatic in the least. Boxes are the most prone to attach themselves to history and **tradition.** They are often into antiques or, at the very least, a more traditional early American look will suffice. Often, boxes recreate their "growing up" environment. Colors of gold, green, and tan interspersed with wooden furniture will please a box. Wall decorations such as trophies, plaques, and symbols of Americana are often found in box homes.

6. Forget the gourmet routine. Boxes are not high risk-takers and this applies to food also. No "flaming apricots" for the box—just good 'ole meat and potatoes will do . . . or mother's great waldorf salad maybe. *Note*: Boxes may become "health food nuts" rather easily; not because it's

in style, but because it makes sense! If this happens, be ready to purchase the food scale and find that remote little health food store, because your box will become compulsive about it. P.S.: When boxes go on diets, they don't need Weight Watchers.® They set their goal and attain it all by themselves!

7. Subscribe to **practical publications** such as *Time*, *Atlantic Monthly*, *Forbes*, and several trade journals in your respective fields. The box wants to be informed and prefers factual, conservative publications. This is the person most prone to read in bed or establish a routine "reading hour" between dinner and the favorite 8 P.M. TV show. Throw out the *People* and the *National Inquirer*; boxes think this is pure silliness. Buy "how-to" manuals, not novels.

8. Make **lists** . . . . of all sorts . . . . about everything. Boxes love to see it in writing because, to them, this reflects an organized mind. Once you have made your list, have a specified place to display it (kitchen bulletin board, refrigerator door, etc.) Boxes need a correct "place" for everything. Don't ever move the box's favorite chair!

Recreation for the Box

1. Forget the "wild" party! Boxes abhor them. The true box *doesn't like social events* in general. Although your box spouse/partner will go when he/she is forced, you need to be prepared to carry the ball in socializing. Expect your box to want to leave early, unless, of course, he/she has found another box to talk with. (Boxes are the ones who talk "shop" at company parties.) If the party is requisite, be sure it is planned weeks ahead. Don't expect your box to be the life of the party; but do expect a thorough analysis of the party on the way home in the car. Don't overindulge. A drunken spouse at the company party is a box's worst nightmare!

2. Choose **friends** carefully. The box likes to stick close to home and does enjoy having a few friends over (one or two couples, max). However, the types of people are important, for the box is choosy about his/her friends. He/she prefers the linear types (boxes, triangles and rectangles). In fact, many boxes gravitate to rectangles to "straighten" out their confusion. Boxes can feel helpful and important in this way. In the social setting, boxes attach themselves to the warmth and understanding of the circle (particularly if the box is in his/her complaining mood). However, boxes are entirely put off by squiggles, believing they're erratic and crazy people!

3. *Do not display affection in public.* In fact, avoid emotional displays of all sorts. The box finds this offensive. Don't worry, your box does love you, and is willing to cuddle at home, but not on the subway!

4. Boxes like **hobbies**. In fact, they often have very elaborate ones: full woodworking shops, separate sewing rooms, etc. Whatever the avoca-

tional choice, the box will approach it with the same attention to detail and organization that is applied to life in general.

5. Boxes prefer **noncompetitive sports**. They often jog, bicycle, and participate in individualistic activities. Boxes may belong to spas or body-building centers. If they must participate in competitive activities, they prefer golf or tennis to racquetball or a team sport. Boxes are often excellent opponents in chess, checkers, or card games such as bridge.

6. For the box, the *ideal vacation is at home*. Boxes are not interested in cruising to exotic places and certainly not in "people watching" at the beach. Boxes often spend their vacation time taking on a new project in the home; two weeks to work on the computer, in the shop, or on the roof is great! Of course, the box will also be the one to make the required trip home to the relatives on his/her summer vacation week. In fact, many boxes have this vacation planned permanently from year to year. They see it as their duty.

7. Forget about mixing business with pleasure. Boxes don't like to take their spouses with them on business trips. Work is work and play is play. Boxes are methodical about separating their personal from their professional lives.

8. During holiday season, the box may surprise you and buy you an expensive gift . . . . like a new washing machine. The box prefers practical gifts, for self and others. Avoid the temptation to buy a box ultrasuede or silk, and certainly discard the notion of that Rolex watch. These showy, impractical things are not appealing to boxes. However, he/she will never miss a birthday or an anniversary. You can count on it!

What to Expect from Your Box

Pluses

1. Consistent, predictable behavior and routine
2. Stable, calm, non-emotional reactions to problems
3. Commitment . . . . "as good as his/her word"
4. Disciplined, hard worker, good provider
5. Respected by you and others for knowledge
6. Serious approach to marriage and parenting
7. Conservative, traditional values and politics
8. Steadfast and dependable in every sense

Minuses

1. Anti-social behavior in large groups
2. Tunnel-vision about his/her beliefs; inflexibility
3. Resistance to change—old ways are best

4. Low risk-taker

5. Over-protective of family; strict parent

6. Possible "tightwad" with money—over-emphasis on saving and security; hoards possessions

7. "Black/white" thinker—fails to see the "grays"—it's wrong or it's right—period!

8. Poor sense of humor

HOW TO "ACCENTUATE THE POSITIVE" IN YOUR BOX

1. Provide a basic, dependable, predictable home environment as a base to make the box feel secure.

2. Be sure the box knows that that he/she is respected and valued by others and *loved* by you.

3. When problems arise, approach your box with unemotional logical and rational suggestions for solutions. Provide *objective data* whenever possible. *Example*: It is far better to state the specific negative actions of the child who requires discipline, than to rant and rave over what a "bad," uncontrollable child he/she has been.

4. Don't push the box to compromise his/her basic values. This will result in a stronger position being taken.

5. Don't surprise your box. Let him/her in on any plans. The box is not comfortable in spontaneous situations.

6. Pay attention to details. Keep records. Put it in writing whenever possible.

7. Do not argue with your box in public. Take it on the chin and wait for a private time. The box is already uncomfortable around others; this is very embarrassing to him/her.

8. Do almost everything in moderation. Boxes respect *self-discipline*. Do not drink, eat, or smoke too much or "go off the deep end" over religion, politics, social issues, etc.

9. Be particularly sensitive to your choice of friends brought into the home. This is sacred turf to the box, and he/she will become upset if unsavory characters invade it.

10. "Save face" for your box when he/she is wrong—if at all possible. Boxes place great stock in being right, and your box will truly appreciate you if you can find a way to end the altercation with a win/win solution for all.

How to Bring Your Box Out of His/Her "Box"

If you will follow the previously set down guidelines, you will have created a **secure relationship** with your box. *Now. . . .* you can begin to make some changes. You must tread lightly, because the box does not change quickly. However, some degree of change is possible if you approach it correctly. I have listed below some typical "desired changes" for the box. If you find one that you agree with, read the approach to take and try it! (*Note*: *If you are a box*, these are excellent suggestions for desirable changes in your behavior that will make your interactions with others more productive.)

1. *Slowly* encourage your box to broaden his/her ability to accept a larger circle of friends. You might begin by solidifying a relationship with one other couple. Then, include another. . . . then, another. When a large party is being given, be sure that at least one other close couple friend will attend with the two of you. Whatever you do, *do not be jealous* of any friendships your box may develop. It is rare enough for him/her to reach out to others. Don't stand in the way!

2. Encourage your box to *listen to other points of view*. This is very difficult, particularly if the box has made a firm decision about something, or if the new view challenges some deeply held beliefs. However, it can be done with patience and by presenting opposing information as **objective data**. In order to succeed here, you must remember the fact that boxes are highly linear and analytic. When confronted with new information, they are capable of processing it thoroughly and changing former views; but the new information must be as sound and logical as the former was. And. . . . you must present the new data **unemotionally**. Also, stress *similarities* in views, not differences.

3. Watch your **timing**. It is best to approach a box *before* he/she has made up his/her mind about something. During the data-collection phase, the box is an excellent listener and will be most open to your perspective. However, once the box has taken a position, he/she can be very *stubborn* about changing it.

4. Create a higher **risk-taking** environment. Boxes tend to maintain the status quo rather than expand, reach out, and try new things. Getting the box to take risks is a difficult assignment. **Start small.** Plan an event which requires some degree of spontaneous behavior; that is, a carnival, a resort week-end. Put the box in a situation where small *spontaneous decisions* must be made. Make sure that the decisions made by the box are supported by you and others. This will help your box to develop confidence in his/ her ability to be spontaneous. Now increase the frequency of these type of

situations: a "last minute" invitation to a party, a "spur of the moment" request to go to the beach or camping.

Each of these experiences (they must be successful) will enhance the box's ability to act spontaneously—thus, to learn that he/she can take a **risk** and it will come out OK! As the confidence level grows, so will the amount and degree of risk-taking. Eventually, the box will agree to investments in "high risk stocks": to calling friends at the last minute to come over; maybe even to consider buying that condo on the beach or changing jobs! These are scary things for boxes to do, since it is outside of their normal behavioral pattern. But with some patience and careful planning on your part, you can begin to bring your box out of his/her box.

5. Develop the **sense of humor.** Boxes do have one, but it is often submerged beneath their tendency to take life (and themselves) too **seriously.** Help your box develop humor by first demonstrating that *you* enjoy people who make you laugh! Next, encourage your box to try some joke-telling. This does not come naturally to boxes, so some initial help from you is required. The early attempts may be horrible. *Laugh anyway!*

A good way to start is for the box to use the "memorized joke" approach. (This is preferred by linears anyway.) You may need to prime him/her with the punchline the first few times. Since the box is heavily left-brained, another humorous technique that seems to work well for boxes is the use of the *pun.* Punning requires an analytical mind which is the box's forte!

6. It's OK to talk about **feelings.** Of the five shapes, the box is the **least** likely to share his/her feelings; the circle is most likely to do so. If you are in a box-circle partnership, this may be the source of many of your problems. Boxes will *avoid direct confrontation* whenever possible. Circles want to get it out in the open and deal with it. Some adjustment is required on the part of both shapes. The circle must learn to present more hard data, thus, giving logical *reasons* for his/her emotion. The box must learn that it's OK to express emotion. It's normal and natural and is *not* a sign of weakness. This is tough for boxes, and you must reinforce the feeling response whenever possible if you want it to continue.

7. Loosening the parental "iron fist" may save your child's mental health. Box parents often become tyrants, so to speak, about *following the rules.* The tendency toward perfection that they apply to themselves somehow gets transferred to the 4 year old who doesn't yet have the self-discipline to abide by the strict rules of the box father/mother. It will be important that you intervene here and soften the situation. Ultimately, it may be useful for the box parent to do some reading on early childhood development. It is also crucial that the box parent does not pull the reins in too tightly during the child's *adolescence.* This is the wrong time to get too tough! I

have known box parents who actually "lost" their children for many years after because they came down too hard on them during the 12 to 16 year old period.

8. Moving the immovable object is difficult, since boxes tend to cling stubbornly to what's right (in their view, of course). Boxes tend to carry a black/white perspective of the world. Helping them to see the gray areas can be of great benefit to you and, ultimately, to them. You may want to read the "Winning an Argument with a Box" section at the beginning of Chapter Four to learn the specific steps in this process.

Overall, the box spouse/partner is a very supportive, stable, and constant companion. Remember . . . . each of the shapes has its weaknesses, but each also has the *capacity to change*. As the box's partner, you have the most direct influence over him/her and can most directly help these changes to occur.

HOW TO FIND A BOX MATE

If you like the way box people sound, you may want to find one for yourself. Or, if you are a box yourself, you may prefer "birds of a feather"—another box as a mate. If so, the following is an itemized list of steps you can take to locate and snare your box. Good luck and happy hunting!

Places to Find Boxes

1. Library
2. In the office, working late or early
3. Computer software stores
4. Brokerage houses
5. CPA firms or accounting departments
6. Meetings of professional organizations (NAA, etc.)
7. Commuting during rush hour
8. Working in banks or for the government
9. Assistant to the top executive (triangle)
10. In the home of a close friend.

What to Say to a Box

1. "Tell me about your job."
2. "Do you have any hobbies?"
3. "Where is your company on the *Fortune* 500 list?"

4. "What are your major problems with your boss?"
5. "Could you advise a good investment for me?"
6. "What are the ingredients in this beer/soda/salad?"
7. "Did you read this morning's *Wall Street Journal*?"
8. "What is your family history/lineage?"
9. "What is your daily work schedule like?"
10. "What does your schedule look like for next Saturday at 8 P.M.?"

What to Do on Your First Date

1. Dress conservatively. Men: Wear a coat and tie or, if the occasion is casual, plain slacks (no jeans) with a clean, crisp white shirt. Women: Dress along the same principle with minimal makeup and jewelry.
2. Plan to attend a serious play or movie. Something that deals with world issues such as Latin America, abortion, minorities, etc. The symphony is even better.
3. Eat at a simple, small, quiet restaurant. Something in good taste with efficient service will do.
4. Avoid including other couples—at least in the beginning.
5. Behave properly. Do not approach your date with any direct or suggestive sexual innuendoes.
6. Apply moderation. Do not drink and eat too much. Do not express yourself with dramatic gestures or intense emotion. Behave in a serious and subdued fashion.

How to Approach the "Sexual Question"

1. Wait until at least the third date to initiate/accept an emotional expression (for example, a kiss).
2. Broach the subject in conversation on the fourth date. Say something like: "I recently read an article in the *New Yorker* that said 85 percent of single men/women must experience sexual intercourse at least twice weekly. What are your views on the subject?"
3. Make your move or accept his move on the fifth date. Be sure the scene is properly set for a quiet evening at your place. Prepare an excellent dinner, turn on the phone recorder, and, whatever you do, don't rush!
4. During the sexual experience, do *not* scream or moan or be overly effusive in any way.
5. When it's over, smile broadly, but say nothing. Later in the evening identify one specific behavior that you were particularly fond of and briefly mention it. Do not rush out.

6. How to "pop the question". . . . Carefully rehearse, then say something like: "I own 'X' cars, homes, bank accounts, credit cards, pets, and cranky relatives. My habits are impeccable—I am neat with few unpleasant mannerisms. Will you marry me? Please sign the contract on the bottom line!"

THE BOX CHILD

Once you have your box spouse, you may soon have a box child also! They tend to be excellent students in school. Their perseverance and self-discipline pay off! However, there are also some built-in problems with box children which need to be addressed here. If the solutions that I offer are unworkable for you, explore other avenues. Please realize, although your child may demonstrate box-like characteristics at this point in his/her life, this is a *child*! He/she will change—probably many times—before reaching adulthood. Guidance from you during this highly malleable period is critical.

Problem 1: Anti-social Behavior. Of all the five shapes, the box has the highest tendency here (the circle the lowest). Although the box will tend to perform well in school and this will make you proud, you also will want to be concerned with your child as a "whole person." Boxes can easily become loners in life and some are happy living their lives in this manner! However, in the school setting, your child will be forced to interact with others and will develop higher self-confidence if this is done with greater ease.

Solution: *Start early* in establishing social interaction with your child and other children. Pre-school is a good idea for box children because it's purpose is to develop social and motor skills with a minimal amount of cognitive development. Avoid early childhood programs designed to develop "geniuses." Your box child will apply adequate pressure to him/herself throughout life; he/she does not need excessive external pressure.

As the child matures, be sure to encourage having friends over to the house, even if it is not always convenient for you. Reinforce a *variety of friends* since boxes tend to be attracted to their own kind. You may find yourself with a bunch of little "eggheads" running around the house. It's good for your box child to befriend a few circles, triangles, and squiggles. They will expand his/her horizons.

Another helpful hint is to encourage your box to become involved in *team sports*. This will enhance the social interaction and fulfill his/her need to belong to a group with an organized purpose. Excellent programs are available for both boys and girls these days, both inside and outside the formal school setting.

Problem 2: Compulsive Behavior. Once boxes lock into something, they are very stubborn about it and often refuse to change. Now, if your box child is compulsive about positive, healthy things—good for you! However, it is possible that he/she may choose something that you are opposed to—something that may do him/her harm (e.g., drugs, unsavory friends, sexual promiscuity). If so, you will want to intervene. How you do it can either release your child from the damaging situation, *or* it can actually solidify the compulsion. Be careful!

Solution: Begin with *preventive action*. This is where the early years are again important. The "programming" of the child is said to occur primarily between the ages of 2 and 6. This is the time the *basic values* are built in. Remember, your child is likely to "do what *you* do . . . . not what you say!" For example, a child who observes his/her parents using drugs when he/she is young, is much more likely to emulate their behavior when he/she comes of age.

Note: Boxes are compulsive. This means that once they take up a line of action, they have difficulty retreating from it. Whereas you as a adult know the correct time and place for a given behavior, you can start and stop at will. This is much more difficult for your child.

Problem 3: Perfectionism. This can be a major stumbling block for box children. They receive reinforcement for it from every corner; teachers are a primary source. If the child falls into this pattern, this will lead to later difficulties in taking chances, risks, and generally trying things in life that he/she doesn't know if he/she can do perfectly. This is a difficult characteristic for parents to see and correct because they tend to be so proud of a job well done!

Solution: Again, if you yourself are a box, you may set the same pattern in your child. First, you must be aware of this and avoid the need to "clone yourself"—for your child's good. Secondly, allow your child to *make mistakes* from an early age. Reinforce "trying it" over "perfecting it." Be confident in the fact that once he/she finds something he/she really likes, he/she will give it full effort. Remember . . . . even excellence is not perfection!

Problem 4: Career Ambivalence. As the box child matures and begins to consider his/her life work (that's the way it's thought of—as work, not achievement), he/she may waffle on a final career. This is a natural outgrowth of the box's tendency to **procrastinate** on the major life decisions. Particularly if you are a triangle, this will be very *frustrating* to you. One day he/she wants to become a pilot, the next, a computer scientist.

Solution: Don't push! Once the box does make a choice, it's engraved in stone. Making the wrong one in a hurry can be very damaging throughout life. Allow the child to *explore many careers*. Introduce him/her to people who work within the fields that he/she is interested in. Also, remember that boxes are most comfortable in a work situation that is structured and well-defined. A list of typical box jobs can be found in Chapter One. This list is not exhaustive, but will give you a good idea of areas toward which to steer your box child.

What to Expect from the Box Child at Home

1. Constant questions! About everything! The box wants to **know**. Why momma? Why daddy? Be ready to answer.

2. Completed homework and a clean room! The ideal kid, right?! Boxes follow the rules. But . . . . be sure this does not become compulsive, perfectionist behavior!

3. One or two close friends. It is unlikely that you will have to have wild parties or a whirlwind social schedule with which you have to keep up.

4. Commitment to tasks. Whatever the box makes a commitment to, he/she will do his/her best to accomplish. Please be clear—this is the box's commitment, not yours!

5. Tells the truth. Unless there is some powerful peer influence during the adolescent period, boxes are not inherently liars. Even if they try, you can easily see through them.

6. Possessive about things. Boxes do not **share** well. Your box will be perfectly comfortable when you write his/her name on the inside label of the camp clothes.

7. Complainer. You won't like this one, but boxes sometimes feel unappreciated. When they do, instead of telling you this outright, they will whine or complain in general. You must encourage the box child to talk directly about what he/she is feeling.

8. Quiet and serious. Personality-wise, this defines the box. Boxes don't take kidding very well. Encourage some playfulness early in life.

How to Raise a Box Child

1. Set down firm guidelines for expected behavior.
2. Establish set routines for meals, bedtime, weekends.
3. Give immediate feedback about task performance.
4. Set the example you want the child to emulate.
5. Create an atmosphere in which the child can *explore* and *make mistakes* without undue recrimination.
6. Communicate clearly at all times.

7. Do not vacillate on decisions.

8. Always give *reasons* for decisions—not "because I said so!"

Overall, box children are pure pleasure. They will do their best to do it right and to make you proud of them. Believe in them and compliment their efforts, and they will do anything for you.

SUMMARY

If you live with a box or two, lucky you. They are hard working, honest, direct, organized, and literal encyclopedias of information. The downside is their tendency to be perfectionist, stubborn, overly serious, and procrastinators.

Of course, we all have a few flaws and these too can be overcome with a bit of patience and "box-like" perseverance. Treat your box with respect; that is the greatest gift you can afford him/her.

Chapter 4

The Box at Work

In this chapter, we will examine together the typical habits and behaviors of the box person in the work setting. As you recall, the box's most characteristic trait is his/her stubbornness. So, we will first look at how the box deals with **conflict.** You will find the section on "How to Win an Argument with a Box" to be very useful if you currently work with a dominant box person.

Next, we will examine the box in different capacities: the box co-worker, boss, and customer. You will find good suggestions here concerning how to deal with boxes on each level. If you will stop and take the time to *analyze each of your work associates* before reading this chapter, it will be more useful to you.

The "typical box jobs" listed in Chapter One were:

accountant	computer programmer/specialist
administrator	bank teller
secretary	government worker
administrative assistant	paper processor
doctor (specialist)	truck driver
manual worker	author/editor
teacher	

However, please be aware that boxes can be found in any line of work. The previous list is not exhaustive; it is merely definitive of jobs and positions that would best suit the dominant traits of a box. This does not mean that there are not numerous other positions that boxes might hold and be very successful in performing. Also remember that *no person is purely one shape.* Although each of us has one dominant shape, each of us also has a *mixture of traits* from the other four shapes. For example: a box with triangle influence is a good manager; a box with circular influence, a better salesperson and parent; a box with squiggle influence, a more effective musician.

Regardless of the job title, if a box finds him/herself in a highly unstructured, confused, disorganized organization or department, he/she will have a problem adjusting. This type situation will be heavily stress-producing for a box. More information about this is available in the next chapter.

HOW BOXES DEAL WITH CONFLICT IN THE WORKPLACE

To begin with, there are five classic, textbook methods of dealing with conflict. Once you know what shape your "difficult person" is, you can quickly determine which **conflict method** he/she is likely to choose.

Five Conflict Styles	*Shape Preferences*
competition	triangle, squiggle
accommodation	circle
avoidance	box, rectangle, squiggle
compromise	circle, triangle
collaboration	circle, box, squiggle, rectangle

Boxes do not like conflict, period! Thus, their strongest tendency is merely to avoid it entirely! In certain situations, this approach is doubtlessly the best choice. However, a certain amount of conflict is a healthy thing for an organization. Out of difference of opinion, more effective solutions are discovered; and when people work together over time, there are bound to be differences of opinion. This simple truth is often submerged in organizations and departments in order to keep the peace.

The reason that boxes avoid conflict is because they dislike emotionally-charged situations among people. Boxes are most uncomfortable expressing emotion. Their preference is a coolly analytical approach to problem-solving. If boxes had their way, everyone would sit around the table taking their turn at spouting off the facts and figures necessary to solve the problem. Suddenly—as if by magic—the solution would appear above their heads! It would be similar to two computers working simultaneously to solve a complicated problem. Certainly no radical human emotion would be involved!

Unfortunately for the box, people are not computers, and group problem-solving rarely goes that smoothly. This is why the box would just as soon *avoid conflict*—have others fight it out and tell him/her the results. (Secretly, the box avoids confrontation partially because he/she is afraid of losing, but the box would never admit this.)

The box is capable of using *collaboration* as a problem-solving technique, as long as the group remains unemotional and each group member is sufficiently qualified and knowledgeable to complete the task.

If you do "corner a box" and find yourself in direct conflict with him/her, the following steps will assist you in getting what you want.

HOW TO WIN AN ARGUMENT WITH A BOX

1. Do not catch the box unprepared to discuss the problem. More than any other shape, boxes must feel totally prepared. This is not a person to stop in the hallway to iron out a problem. Boxes are not spontaneous people.

2. Think through your argument thoroughly before you approach your box adversary. *Do your homework*! Rest assured that the box will do his/hers.

3. Research not only your own proposal, but that of the box as well. The more successful debator knows as much about the opponent's side as his/her own.

4. Be equipped with *hard data*. Facts and figures—not emotional appeals—are convincing to boxes. **Use logos** (logic), **not ethos** (emotion) with boxes.

5. Put it in *writing*. It will carry more credibility with a box if it's set down in the printed word. Boxes don't trust face-to-face communication. (This is because they are not sensitive to body language, and often miss the subtle cues of the opponent.) Send the box a full *written report*.

6. Send the report in advance. Boxes are not swift decision-makers. However, once they decide, they are firm about their decision. You must give the box *time* to think about it. If your timing is right, you will present your proposal *before* the box has already made up his/her mind. If not, sending the report in advance is even more important because the box will take an even longer time to reverse a decision already made.

7. Make an appointment. After you have given the box sufficient time to ponder your point of view (report), it is time to discuss it one-to-one. Follow proper procedures here. Do not approach the discussion casually.

8. Plan to hold at least three sessions to discuss the matter. The box will not make a decision the first time. It will take several sessions and discussions to arrive at a final conclusion. Be prepared for this. The box is very *patient*; you must be too.

9. Use the first session as a *listening period*. Let the box do the talking, but take notes! The box will shoot holes in your proposal and, in doing so, give away his/her information that is contrary to yours.

10. Prepare for the second session by designing your argument based on the logic of the box. (You learned this in the first session when you

were listening so carefully.) Find new data to counter the box's data. Ideally, find new information that the box is unaware of. Be sure your information is accurate. You can't put one over on a box.

11. Although you will probably convince the box in the second session, the decision will not likely come until the third. When the box does finally bow to your side, don't gloat!

12. Save face for the loser. Boxes are concerned with maintaining the *respect* of their colleagues. Whatever you do, do not demean the box for losing the argument. Boxes will give in to the facts and figures—not to people. You won because you did your homework, and the box can admit that without losing face. Remember, you may be the loser the next time.

THE BOX CO-WORKER

Co-workers and colleagues (university version of same) come in all sizes and *shapes*. If you have a box or two in your office, it will behoove you to more fully understand why they behave as they do. The following are some typical behaviors displayed by boxes in the work setting. When you recognize a certain behavior, the reason for it will become clear to you.

Each of these typical behaviors can cause a problem for co-workers, thus, solutions are offered to help you.

Problem 1: "The policy clearly states . . . ." Boxes go *by the book*. Furthermore, they know the book by memory. It is not unusual to find copies of the personnel policy, practice, and procedure manuals on the shelf above the box's desk.

Solution: This is an *exception* to the rule. The policy is intended as a guideline, not as a hard and fast rule. There will always be exceptions and certainly personnel is aware of this.

Problem 2: "We've always done it this way." Boxes maintain the status quo; they are threatened by change.

Solution: This new method will improve our efficiency. My analysis indicates a 12 percent increase in departmental productivity over the next two quarters. (Facts and figures do work with boxes!)

Problem 3: "I'd like to help you, but I'm snowed under!" Boxes do not react well to spur-of-the-moment requests. They follow a daily schedule and meticulously organize their work.

Solution: Do not surprise the box. Plan for the box's involvement ahead of time, and garner his/her agreement. If the interruption is necessary, you may need a higher authority to change the box's priorities.

Problem 4: "I'd like to join you, but I'd miss my deadline!" Whether the invitation is for lunch or a meeting with the project team, the box places his/her own work ahead of any team interaction—particularly a last minute meeting.

Solution: Demonstrate to the box that there is much to be learned by working with others. (Give the box a good book to read on team or synergism.) When the box does agree to go along, ask for his/her opinion, listen, and show respect for his/her contribution. Slowly the box will develop a feeling of belonging and the teamwork will increase.

Problem 5: "It sounds good, but I'd like to see the final figures." Boxes always need more data.

Solution: Give it to them. Bury them under it. Do not expect a box to support a "knee-jerk" decision.

Problem 6: "Sorry . . . . that's not my job." The box is very clear about his/her area of responsibility. He/she has read the job description and has committed it to memory. This, plus the fact that boxes are not the most helpful to others among the five shapes.

Solution: "Would you be willing to tell me the name and phone number of the employee whose job this *is?*" "Could you kindly transfer me to him/her now?"

Problem 7: "I've got too much to do . . . . no one else works as much as me!" This is a typical statement of a box who has been working too hard and doesn't feel *appreciated* by the other office workers. Occasionally, boxes need a little "atta boy/girl" too!

Solution: "You do such a good job, John! What would we do without you around here?" Pat him/her on the back and send him/her back to the cubicle with a smile.

Problem 8: "I can't do any more until I get the report from quality assurance." Boxes believe in a definite flow and organization to the work. If things get gummed up, they are stymied.

Solution: Encourage the box to be creative. Suggest a tangential project that he/she might work on. Divert his/her attention to another area of concern.

Problem 9: "Everyone has gone crazy around here!" This is a typical box statement when the office is experiencing a crisis and people are reacting emotionally. The box is feeling emotional also, but can't admit it, and as a result, blames the others.

Solution: Ask the box how he/she is *feeling* about the situation. This will force the box to take responsibility for his/her own feelings rather than being critical of those feelings of others. It may also help the box to learn that expressing emotion is an acceptable human behavior.

Problem 10: Silence. This is the worst of all. When it gets *really bad,* the box withdraws completely. Boxes have been known not to talk to anybody for days!

Solution: Try and try again. When you're about to give up, go into the box's office, sit down, and just be silent along with him/her. This often results in both of you laughing and the box realizing that being a martyr doesn't cut it. We all need people—even the box—once in awhile.

Overall, the box co-worker is a pretty fine luck of the draw for anyone. This person will certainly pull his/her own weight. You will learn to respect your box's dedication to the task, and you'll love his/her attention to detail. No rock will be left unturned! For all his/her faults (and we all have a few), you'll appreciate a box co-worker much more than someone who doesn't get the job done when others are depending on it.

THE BOX BOSS

Although the box is the *least chosen shape* of all five (see Appendix for database), the majority of people in the work world are required to perform "box jobs." Job descriptions abound in corporations and the government. Each one specifies exactly what tasks are to be performed by each job title in the organization. Heaven forbid that some employee would be in an office somewhere doing something that we didn't know about!

Since the days of Taylor's theory and structure of management, the emphasis in traditional organizations has been less on quality of work and more on *quantity* of work. Of course, a large cause for this is the measurability of both. It's much easier to measure quantity than quality. Thus, how much you do, not how well you do it, is stressed. We are all boxes trying to meet management's quota!

Given this premise, those who do the most work get rewarded. And what is the reward? Sometimes money. But when you reach the top of your pay scale, that's no incentive anymore. So, what's next? A promotion to supervision or management, of course! Now you are "The BOSS!"

Of course, once you become the boss, you continue to do the things that you were rewarded for as a worker—only more of it! Not only does the boss work harder, but he/she insists that the employees work harder also. Harder does not necessarily mean smarter. However, in organizations where quantity is most important, that doesn't seem to matter. Just "get the work out!"

Bottom line: Bosses often continue to be the same boxes they were as workers. Although their title leads them to believe that they are a *triangle* now, their behavior is largely box-like. "Get the job done" is the motto.

"Don't goof-up this one."

"Follow the rules."

"Read the policy manual."

"Meet the deadline!"

There are pluses and minuses to each of the five shapes in a leadership position. Here are those for a box boss:

Pluses

1. Detailed instructions given to employees with little room for misunderstanding
2. Clear delineation of responsibilities for all
3. Detailed performance feedback; you know where you stand with a box boss
4. Cool and calm in crisis
5. Highly knowledgeable about the job function, often with years of experience on the job

Minuses

1. Slow to make final decisions; they must be prodded
2. Excessive attention to minute details of work
3. Overemphasis on paperwork; they generate excessive forms and reports to prove in value (CYA mentality)
4. Politically naive; they do not represent the department well to higher authority. Refusal to blow own horn; the work is proof enough
5. "All work . . . . no play" philosophy. Although the work gets done, it's not much fun!

How to Please Your Box Boss

1. Do your job!
2. Meet all **deadlines**; even be early on some.
3. Memorize the policy manuals.
4. Take notes when the boss speaks.
5. Keep the boss **informed**—in **writing**. Submit a report in advance to any discussion on the topic.
6. Pay attention to **detail**. Be sure your "t's" are crossed and your margins straight. No typos!
7. Be to work **on time**. However, you are not expected to work late; you'll get home on time too.
8. Establish yourself as a **dependable** member of the team.
9. Do not insist that changes occur overnight; they may not happen at all with a box boss.
10. Show **respect** at all times. This is very important to boxes.

11. Use **formality**. Make appointments. Dress appropriately, and be aware of small things like table manners; the box is. No personal phone calls!

12. Last, but highly *important*, always **support your box boss in front of his/her superiors.** You can grumble among the troops (boxes aren't tuned into the grapevine), but never go over the box's head; that's suicide!

Overall, you could do worse than a box boss. You will know where you stand at all times. You will be clear about your job responsibilities. Although interaction with the boss and performance feedback will be **infrequent** (and never casual), when it does occur, you will learn something. Although the box is basically quiet, when he/she does talk, there is something important to say.

THE BOX CUSTOMER

It occurred to me that it might be useful to some of my readers to spend a few paragraphs describing a typical box customer. Since America is currently experiencing a "renewed" emphasis on *customer service*, the identification of your customer within the five shapes could certainly assist you in knowing how to approach this person. Ultimately, this short section might be a future money maker for you if you are in a sales or customer service job.

As you read this section, think of your current customers. Identify someone whom you feel is a box. Maybe this is someone you have difficulty with. This section will help you interact more effectively with this box customer, and others in the future.

How to Identify a Box Customer

1. Appearance will be very businesslike—conservative suit, still crisp looking at 5 P.M.

2. Purposeful movement. Unrushed and fluid as he/she examines your merchandise.

3. Facial expression will be a frown or a poker face.

4. He/she will not touch the merchandise immediately, fearful of claiming early ownership.

5. Questions will be very **specific** and in pursuit of details about the product or service.

6. Cost/pricing will be asked within the first few questions.

7. Questions will demonstrate prior knowledge of your product. Boxes read *Consumer Report* before they shop.

8. A demonstration will be appreciated.

9. Do *not* use a "hard sell" approach. This will send him/her to your competitor fast.

10. Do not expect a **quick sell**; the box has to go home and think about it. Expect comparison shopping.

How to "Sell" a Box Customer

1. Be serious. A firm handshake will suffice as a greeting. No personality stuff. The box is there to buy, not to befriend you. Use direct eye contact. Don't smile much.

2. Give detailed info. Methodically list all the benefits and features. Boxes will even want to see the owner's manual graphs if possible. This customer is a test of your knowledge of your product/service. If you can't handle it, pass him/her on to someone who can. *Don't ever lie to a box!*

3. Don't talk too much. With boxes, there are often uncomfortable periods of silence. He/she is thinking. Do not disturb.

4. Don't probe into the box's personal life/habits. Boxes are private people and this is offensive to them.

5. Don't rush around. Keep your posture erect and your body quiet. Imitate the movement (or lack thereof) of the customer. Quick movements make boxes distrust you.

6. Whatever you do, don't push for the "sell" too soon. In fact, you are better off not to do this at all! Just accept the fact that this customer is not an impulse buyer. However, if you do the things listed above, and your product is of quality, the box will be back to buy.

7. Always give a box customer some printed matter to take away. A flyer, brochure or business card are things to show the tangible result of his/her effort.

8. If the box is an ongoing customer of yours, expect to hear from him/her immediately when something goes wrong. Don't worry, the box is not a screamer! Your box customer will give you a thorough description of the problem in a very clinical manner. It will then be up to you to fix it. You'd better, or the box will take it further. Boxes are the "letter-writers" of the world, and they are not adverse to writing directly to your Chairman of the Board. Keeping a box customer happy is really very simple: just do your job and don't make any promises that you can't keep!

SUMMARY

When all is said and done, companies could not function without their boxes. It is compulsory to the organization's success to have a good number of boxes in the workforce. Why? Because boxes get the job done! They are the **hard workers** among us. They are **organized, methodical, efficient, dependable, persevering,** and highly **knowledgeable** in their chosen field.

Their personalities are lackluster when it comes to motivating others or being the life of the party. But, you will always know where you stand with a box, and when the box has something to say, it is wise to listen. Although the box does not talk a lot, when he/she does, the information is very specific.

Box co-workers are highly dependable and you can trust their word when they say they will complete a task. However, they are not the ones to invite for a beer after work. They wouldn't go anyway, since they are conscientious about their responsibilities at home also.

Box bosses are the clearest in their instructions to employees but the most removed from daily office chit-chat. If you want to talk to your box boss, prepare your outline, make an appointment, and stay within your allotted time. The organizations under box leadership are highly productive. They aren't very creative, and they accept change slowly, however. If they are in a stable industry, they will be successful.

You can spot **box customers** a mile away. No matter how hard you try, they will rarely buy on the first visit. However, if you do your homework and if you have a quality product/service, the box will be back.

If you are in **conflict** with a box, review the 12 steps in "Winning an Argument with a Box." They're very useful.

This country was developed by the hard work and sweat of the brow of boxes. We tend to underrate them and that is unfortunate, because we owe them a great debt. If you have a box toiling by your side, shoulder-to-shoulder everyday at work, you are indeed fortunate.

Chapter 5

The Box Under Stress

A natural outgrowth of modern American living is the emergence of human *stress*. All through the late 1970s, into the early 1980s, companies offered programs and workshops on stress management and stress reduction. Many larger corporations created in-house fitness centers to assist their employees (only management in the early days). Why did they do all of this? It wasn't for humanitarian reasons; it was to save money, of course. Consultants demonstrated the damaging effects of stress on the workforce and its impact upon the company through *absenteeism* and *lower productivity*. This is when management sat up and took notice!

Today, it is commonplace for people to discuss their stress level at the most casual cocktail party or gathering of friends. Because there is so much concern about this topic, it seemed only fitting to devote at least a brief chapter to the subject of stress as it relates directly to each one of the five shapes. If you are a box, or are involved directly with a box, this chapter may be very important to you.

Please note: *Not all stress is bad*. Each of us needs a certain amount of tension in our lives to be healthy, productive human creatures. When there is too much, it's bad.

How to Identify a Box Under Stress

1. Disorganization. This is the first real giveaway for the box who is usually highly organized.

2. Disorientation. If the box seems "confused" about what's going on, this is a good indicator of stress.

3. Nervousness. Boxes are normally solid and stable individuals. If he/she starts to fiddle with pens, develop twitches or new mannerisms, this is a sign.

4. **Forgetfulness.** This is a good sign for a box under stress because it is very rare in this shape.

5. **Erratic Body Movements.** The box is usually calm, controlled, and smooth in body movement and gesture. If these become jerky or clumsy it is an indicator.

6. **Indecision.** Although the box is not known as a quick decision-maker, under stress he/she will have difficulty with even the simplest, everyday decisions.

7. **Insomnia.** More than any other shape, this will emerge in a box under stress. Watch for it.

8. **Social Flamboyance.** This is highly unusual behavior for boxes. If you suddenly find your box "hanging from the chandelier" at the party, you know something is amiss!

9. **Excessiveness.** If he/she starts to drink, eat, or smoke too much—or even to overdo things usually done in moderation—make note. Also, take note if he/she is overly **negative** about things.

10. **Changing Mind.** Once boxes make a decision, they rarely renege on it without a great deal of consideration and reflection. If your box is suddenly reversing decisions at a moment's notice, something is wrong.

Note: A final indicator is an *intensification of the box's negative traits*: meticulous, nit-picking, procrastinating, aloof, resistant to change, complaining, and working alone. In normal times, the box can balance these traits with his/her positive characteristics. Under stress, these traits will emerge and magnify.

Sources of Stress for Boxes

1. **The Wrong Job.** This is the number one cause of stress for boxes. Boxes *must* be satisfied in their work because their work is the focus of their lives. Boxes need jobs that have specific descriptions and requirements. They must know what is expected of them and why. They need to be placed in highly structured situations involving repetitive tasks and routines.

When these things are not true, the box becomes convoluted. If they live in a work environment that is prone to "management by crisis"—if the right hand doesn't know what the left hand is doing—the box is in trouble.

2. **Disorganization.** At home or at work, if everything suddenly goes "topsy-turvy," the box will experience temporary stress. For example: a change of management at work, a shift in job responsibilities, a change of office location, a move to another city or house. If the situation becomes stabilized rather quickly, the box will return to normalcy. However, if it takes awhile for the dust to settle, the box's stress will increase.

3. Social Requirements. Remember, this is not the box's forte. It is all the box can do to make it to the annual company Christmas party! Then he/she wants to leave early. If the box is in a situation where extensive hosting of social events is required, this is highly stressful. (This is one reason why many boxes are rejected from the upper executive ranks, where lavish entertaining is often a norm.)

4. Co-workers. The box prefers to work alone, and when forced to interact extensively with co-workers, he/she is uncomfortable to begin with. Now . . . . if the co-workers are inexperienced, unqualified, or just downright ignorant or lazy, the box is intolerant. After all, the box works hard and he/she expects others to do the same! (The box is not a good person to assign to break in a new employee. Unless the "new baby" is a quick study, the box will become unenamored quickly.)

5. Parenting Problems. An unruly child is unacceptable to a box parent. Boxes carefully plan the child-rearing period. They read books, establish routines, and analytically prepare for each phase of the child's development. When something goes wrong, they feel totally at a loss! The worst period in any child's development tends to be *adolescence*. This period may throw the box parent for a loop! No textbook can thoroughly prepare one for the offspring who suddenly thinks mom and dad are stupid idiots!

6. Relationship Problems. This is last on the list, purposefully. Since boxes are the least concerned with people, it is the last crisis to really bother them. In fact, the box spouse is often literally the last to know when the marriage is floundering. The spouse may have tried to *talk about it* again and again, but boxes don't like discussing feelings and tend to slough off such conversations.

Boxes tend to take personal relationships *for granted*. This is a major problem, because when they finally realize that there are serious problems, it hits like a ton of bricks. The sudden shock will send the otherwise stable box into a tailspin. If the marital/relationship problem occurs in conjunction with a major work-related change, the box is in need of some serious help.

Stressful People for Boxes

Now let's examine what types of people tend to cause the box the most stress. You can apply your own knowledge of the characteristics of the other four shapes here. You will arrive at similar conclusions to those listed below.

As you read this section, think of the significant others in the life of your box. Does he/she have to work with or live with a squiggle? If so, there are automatic problems in their relationship.

Please note: There is a school of thinking which postulates the notion that "opposites attract"! Apparently, there is some truth in this, because we have all met couples who seemed to be *direct opposites*, yet who appeared to have an excellent relationship. This seems to be particularly true in a love relationship. Where the box would have difficulty *working with a squiggle*, he/she might enjoy the **balance** of this opposite shape in his/her personal life.

1. Squiggles. This is the most *opposite* shape to the box. Read Section Five on the squiggle for full details. The major problem with squiggles is their lack of attention to detail, their disorganization, and their highly changeable personality. The box prefers people who are consistent and dependable. Squiggle traits (at least in the workplace) are unacceptable.

2. Circles. The second *right-brained* shape can also wreak havoc on a box. Circle's main concern is *people*. The box's main concern is the *work*. Boxes cannot understand why circle people are always so concerned about how everybody feels about it! The box thinks we should just comply and get the job done. The circle is also prone to want to *discuss* everything and the box remains a quiet, private person. Boxes often describe circles as "overpersonal" or "flaky."

3. Rectangles. Boxes and rectangles have a sort of love/hate relationship. At first meeting, the box is put off by the confusion and ambivalence of the rectangle. However, if the rectangle will come to the box for *advice*, the box will enjoy the opportunity to share his/her knowledge with this neophyte and learn to appreciate the rectangle more. Boxes can be excellent *teachers* when they choose to be. The rectangle is in a state of transition and change, and because of this, most open to new learning. Thus, rectangles can make ready pupils for willing box teachers. (More in Section Three.)

4. Triangles. In most situations, the box and triangle are an *excellent match*. They are both left-brained and analytical. They both share a need to know the rules and live in a structured environment. Boxes are the one shape that does the best job of *taking orders from the triangle* (see Section Two).

The problem comes when the triangle envisions him/herself as a **change agent**. Triangles are most often found in positions above boxes in the chain of command. In fact, they are often the "commanding officer" to whom the box reports. In this capacity, it is sometimes necessary for the triangle boss to make major changes in the work objectives or flow. Unless the triangle takes the time to *explain the changes* carefully to the troops, confusion and mutiny may occur. This is when the box experiences direct conflict with the triangle.

It is worth mentioning that a second point of conflict between boxes and triangles is their method of resolving conflict. Where boxes have a tendency to *avoid conflict*—hoping it will go away—triangles choose *competition* and go for a win/lose solution through *direct confrontation*. The box will almost always lose in this situation. After having lost too many times to the more powerful triangle, the box will eventually build resentment and hostility toward him/her. This will erode their past ability to work together well.

Note: The most typical shape combo in the workplace is triangle/box. These two individuals tend to make the best team and—as long as the triangle is the boss—they are highly productive together. The triangle gives the orders; the box carries them out. As long as this is clear, stress will be minimal between boxes and triangles.

How the Box Deals with Stress

1. **Recognition.** The first and most important step is recognition. Boxes tend to bury themselves in their work and are often unaware of their own stress. It is the *disorganization* they experience that will first bring it to their attention. Once the box is *willing to admit it*, the following stages may develop in the box's attempt to handle his/her stress. Some are positive approaches, some not. All are typical of boxes.

2. **Workaholism.** This is the most natural reaction of the box. Because his/her focus in life is work, when the going gets tough, he/she tends to turn up the heat and work harder. Of course, this is a poor solution to stress reduction, but it will work for awhile for a box!

3. **Withdrawal.** Since the box has a tendency to be a loner anyway, this is also a natural reaction. The problem is that this is the very time the box needs the support and understanding of others. The box must be forced to talk about it, as is explained in the next section.

4. **Study.** If the box has truly admitted that he/she is experiencing stress, then one of his/her most natural behaviors is to learn as much as possible about this thing called "stress." More than any of the other four shapes, it is the box who will attend the stress management courses, buy the stress reduction tapes, and spend hours in the library doing research on stress. Although these are positive solutions, this will not solve the problem. The box will end up knowing more about stress than anyone else, but will not make the life decisions to alleviate it!

5. **Depression . . . .** will set in over time. The box prides him/herself in always being in control. The more stress takes over, the more the self-confidence of the box is eroded. When the box gets down enough on him/herself, he/she may just give up. This is when some serious, professional help must be sought. It is no longer sufficient to rely on friends and family. The problem is too severe now.

Please note: Before you run off and make an appointment with a psychiatrist, please understand that *full depression is fairly rare*. This does not happen immediately during or even after a highly stressful life event. Depression does not usually occur until many months, and even years after a *series of crises*. Just one traumatic event doesn't cause depression for most people. Although we all talk about being *depressed* about something, true depression is a very serious psychological *and* physical illness. What your box may really need is temporary help from a professional counselor. This is called **crisis intervention.** Often, family and friends can provide this service *if* the person in stress is willing to allow them to help!

How to Help Your Box to Reduce Stress

1. **Talk About It!** This is a tall order with a box, but it must be done! You may be vaguely aware that your box's behavior has changed. You may have identified four or five things in the list of indicators at the beginning of this chapter. However, you may be at a loss to know the *reason for the stress*. In fact, your box may not know either. Often, by talking it over with another concerned person, the source of the stress will become clear. Stress reduction begins with knowledge and admission of stress. Without this, the rest is unimportant.

2. **Explore Alternatives.** Once you have gotten your box to admit his/her stress, you can begin to reduce it together. *The most likely source of stress for boxes is at work.* If this is true, help the box to explore other job possibilities. This is particularly difficult for boxes because they place such emphasis on security and are loath to give up their hard-earned benefit and retirement income!

You must point out the long-term benefits of correct job placement, both financially and personally. If the box is in the wrong job, he/she will not make the quality contribution that he/she is capable of. His/her salary will reflect this deficiency over time. Of course, if your box dies of a stress-related disease such as heart attack, it won't matter!

3. **Outside Activities.** If the opportunities to change jobs are particularly sparse at the moment, it may help to focus the energy of the box on other activities. This may be a good time to take up that new project at home; try the most difficult hobby; buy a new pet; take a trip; join that bowling league the neighbors were talking about. Re-direct the box's energy into something different in which he/she can succeed.

4. **Physical Exercise.** This is one of the proven methods of dealing with stress for many people. Since the box tends to prefer individual athletic endeavors, encourage your box to increase his/her jogging, walking, bicycling schedule during this period. Even consider joining that health spa!

5. **Focus on Homelife.** Particularly if the stress is work-related, this

is a time to let the box withdraw into the comfort and support of his/her loved ones at home. Make an extra effort to prepare favorite foods and schedule favorite activities. Try to be sure that family members are at home and available during times when the box may feel like talking or is merely in need of human company.

6. Get Professional Help. Of all the five shapes, the box will be most appreciative of the advice of a professional. Boxes respect knowledge, and this is a source of information about what the box is experiencing. This will also force the box to talk about it, where he/she may not open up with others. As mentioned in my discussion of depression, it is best to use this method early as *crisis intervention* rather than to wait until the stress causes serious damage in the form of full depression or a stress-related disease.

Boxes feel Most Comfortable When . . . .

1. Everything is on schedule and according to plan.
2. Everyone is in the right place, at the right time, doing the right job.
3. Everyone knows what is expected of him/her and is willing to do it.
4. There are no surprises, no crises, no chaos.
5. There are a minimum of emotional people to have to deal with.
6. The homefront is smooth and predictable; there are established routines and financial security.
7. Everyone recognizes the **hard work** and **contribution** of our box!

Then . . . . "God's in his heaven and all's well with the world!

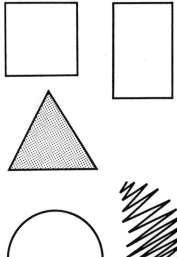

Section Two

THE INTREPID TRIANGLE

Chapter 6

Identifying the Triangle . . . .
_____ How Could You Miss?

Belief: "God helps those who help themselves!"
Translation: Do it now!

You triangles like to **get to the point,** so I will attempt to "tell it like it is" in this section. Like the other four shapes, you triangles have your share of both positive and negative qualities. But, unlike the other shapes, you will tend to see what you want to see in what you are reading. I want to caution you to pay close attention to the _negative traits,_ also, as these will help you understand yourself better. And, if you will listen and take it to heart, you are thoroughly capable of _improving_ in the areas of your shortcomings which will enable you to communicate more effectively with friends and co-workers.

OVERVIEW

"Just a cut above the others" is the theme of the triangle. This shape symbolizes **leadership** and many triangles feel a sense of **destiny** within them: they are "fated" to succeed! Although this life script is invigorating, the downside of this attitude is often an **ambitious** self-centeredness that can run roughshod over anyone who gets in the triangle's way!

The triangle has the ability to be quickly **decisive** at both home and work. This is a very sure person who wants to be right above all! This driving need to be right and to **control** things makes the triangle very **competitive.** These people want to win, and it must be done their way! Because others are not often as confident as they, triangles often do win and are most likely found in positions of authority, or they are on their way to the top!

Triangles do not like to be wrong and have trouble admitting it if they are. They don't like to reverse their decisions and often fail to involve others in decision-making. They are **bottom-line** oriented and quick to get to the point. Triangles have difficulty with people who vacillate on decisions. Triangles say, "either __ or get off the pot!"

Probably the strongest attribute of the triangle person is his/her ability to **focus**. Triangles don't get sidetracked. They are **driven, athletic** personalities who set goals and achieve them! Just get out of their way!

QUICK INDICATORS OF TRIANGLE PEOPLE

Language

Common Words: escalate, interface, re-position, ROI, thrust, smart, reorganization, numbers, percentages, expletives, any current jargon or buzz words.

Common Sayings: "More bang for the buck!" "Get to the point!" "What's in it for me?" "Carry the ball on this one." "We've got a 60/40 chance." "The buck stops here!" "You're FIRED!"

Appearance

Men: Always appropriate for the situation—in a very calculated manner. Although he perceives himself as a "man's man" (athletics, et al) and basically thinks this is a "waste of time," he knows it is important for his image. Higher level triangles have personal tailors; middle level and beginners, at least a favorite salesman in the best men's store in town. The triangle attempts to be stylish without seeming faddish. He prefers the high quality garments such as Hart, Schaffner, and Marks and Florsheim wing-tipped shoes. However, on occasion, the triangle will wear a pastel colored shirt if "all the other guys are doing it." His goal is to look relaxed and casual, even in his $1,000 suit. He carries only the most expensive briefcase, Cross pens, and linen handkerchiefs.

Triangles never want to be caught unprepared. They carry every type of "plastic" invented, plus membership cards to all the private clubs and Frequent Flyer programs. A $100 bill is tucked into the back flap of the wallet for the sake of making an impression on a mogul new to town. Triangles do not carry daily calendars; their box "lieutenant" does this for them. A book of important telephone numbers is handy though. Triangles keep receipts from all business lunches for tax purposes. The more flamboyant ones will sport a decorative college ring or a nice gold and onyx ring, and a Rolex watch, of course. Those with a background in sales may wear the big diamond ring.

Women: (1) "On the way up" women wear suits with tailored cut and conservative colors. Skirts are long and straight; no mini-skirts for this career-minded gal (*Dress for Success* is her Bible). The blouse is high-necked and the shoes plain pumps with medium heels. There is a minimum of makeup and jewelry (18 carat gold, of course). The nails are short and well-manicured, and the perfume is very *au courant*. No purse is carried; the eel briefcase does it all.

(2) "Arrived" women no longer have to play by the rules and often appear in more classically feminine looks; pastel tailored dresses with flowing skirts; expensive decorative pins; open-toe heels; clutch purse or handbag; slightly dangling earrings; open neck blouse; soft colorful scarf. Usually the "arrived woman" is a bit older, thus, a face lift is a possibility with this shape. If the truth were known, both male and female are prone to "color away the gray"!

Office

The office environment is *full of status symbols*, everywhere you look, only the best for the upwardly-striving triangle. All of the classic studies apply here: large square-footage, top floor, glass on two side walls, oversized desk, full couch, separate living quarters attached, private entrance and doorway leading to the boardroom (for the triangle CEO).

The walls are decorated with whatever the triangle feels will illustrate *power* in his/her environment. Look for awards, degrees, certificates, pictures of the plant ground breaking, Chamber of Commerce membership, Little League sponsorship, and trophies from other battlegrounds: hunting, fishing, chess, etc. There will be a few personal effects—a photo with the spouse on the Fjords cruise and one with the latest Governor shaking hands at the last reception in his/her honor. There is little evidence of paperwork to do (not displayed for others to see)—just an OAG flight guide on the desk and a set of the *Harvard Business Review* on the shelf.

Triangular women will keep with the major themes here, but often use lighter colors: light burled wood or glass desk tops with a marble or leather desk set. Men's offices may sport some recent electronic invention: an international time monitor, a laser decision maker, etc. Of course, both offices are heavily guarded by the secretaries who sit outside the door.

Personal Habits

1. **Early Arriver.** It is not enough for a triangle to be prompt, he/she must get there first in order to "scope" the situation and take the best seat.

2. **Fidgety.** If the meeting is long and the boxes are rambling over detailed information, the triangle gets very fidgety. He/she thinks they should "$#%$@ or get off the pot!"

3. **Interrupter.** Manners are unimportant when there's work to be done and these "idiots" need leadership. The triangle will even *finish your sentence for you* in order to get on with it!

4. **Power Handshake.** Triangles learn this one from daddy at about age 8. The triangle's left hand goes *on top* of the two shaking hands to demonstrate superiority.

5. **Addiction.** Because triangles live in the "fast lane," they are prone to *compulsive behavior* and often drink or smoke too much.

6. **Game Player.** This "Type A" personality loves any game as long as he/she has a chance to WIN. From tennis, golf, racquetball to bridge or poker, you name it.

7. **Joke Teller.** The triangle loves the latest joke, and rehearses so that the telling is perfect; there is no forgetting the punchline for a triangle.

8. **Voracious Reader.** The triangle always wants to be on top of it, thus, he/she reads and stays informed about everything from the innerworkings of his/her competitor to the latest Broadway hits. This person subscribes to *GQ* or *Savvy, Fortune, Forbes, Harvard Business Review*, and the Naisbitt *Trend Letter*. In a rare moment of personal reading pleasure, the triangle reads biographies of famous hero role models.

9. **Plays Hard; Works Hard.** This is a motto of the triangle who can be a superb host and entertain lavishly at home. He/she can drink you under the table and be alert the next morning at the 7 A.M. meeting. Don't try to play unless you can keep up.

10. **Prefers Small Groups.** One-to-one communication is preferable over large groups. Although the triangle can be an excellent speaker in front of a large gathering, he/she prefers to persuade people in small numbers at a time.

Body Language

1. **Composed.** Always. The triangle will never let you know that his/her stomach is churning with fury in a meeting.

2. **Jaunty, Large Steps.** The triangle is a sure person, and this is reflected in the walk.

3. Piercing Eyes. Beyond 80 percent eye contact, if interested; less than 50 percent, if not. This is a direct outgrowth of the triangle's ability to *focus* energy.

4. Tensely Pursed Mouth. Particularly under pressure, the triangle demonstrates his/her tension.

5. Large, Sweeping Gestures. The triangle likes to call attention to him/herself. Gestures are few, but purposeful and definite.

6. Power Voice. The volume, rate, and pitch of the voice are de-escalated. The low pitch carries the authority. When under pressure, the volume is softer so others must strain to hear and the rate is slow for emphasis.

7. Smooth Body Movement. The body moves in fluid, smooth waves to indicate full *control* without a sense of hurry or hesitation.

8. Mesomorphic Body Shape. I have often noticed that the more successful triangles share the anthropological mesomorphic body shape. This means they tend to be tall, thin, and of athletic build.

Important Note: What Triangles Must Learn in Life

If you are a triangle, or if there is one in your life, you may want to take heed of these next paragraphs. Of all the five shapes, the triangle can run roughshod over others and *bulldoze* his/her way through life. Why me, you say?

Many of the societal messages we receive as children reinforce and even glorify the triangle. Many people perceive themselves to be triangles when, in fact, they are *boxes in triangle clothing*. Or, many may strive to become triangles who are truly better suited to other types of work and human endeavor. We cannot all be the chiefs; we need a few Indians also. The majority of us are not chiefs, in fact.

Triangle people are the *movers and shakers* in this world. They take the risks, they go out on the limbs for the rest of us. For this, we owe them a great deal. However, they often do so at great personal cost, for the triangle is often a compulsive, ego-centered individual who sometimes finds him/herself alone and unhappy in the waning years of life.

This can be prevented if the triangle can learn to *listen* more to the point of view of others and to *lose* once in awhile so that another may win. The triangle will challenge you and stimulate you to do things you never thought possible. And . . . . he/she is even tougher on him/herself! A triangle will make others sit up and take notice—to learn and grow. The triangle must take his/her own medicine and *learn from others* as well!

SUMMARY

Triangle people are truly few and far between. It is clear that many who choose the triangle may aspire to be triangles, but are really *not* triangles.

True triangles have a life history of radically changing everything and everyone with whom they come in contact. Both personally and professionally, they are swift **decision-makers, competitive, ambitious, athletic** and never happy with the status quo. If there is not a problem, the triangle will create one!

The "secret weapon" of the triangle is his/her ability to **focus** his/her energy on the goal at the moment. Even more astounding is the triangle's ability to shift focus quickly from goal to goal. This is a result of a **quick mind** that functions primarily within the left hemisphere (linear). They become frustrated when others can't keep up with them, and many cannot.

Triangles must learn to work with others in this world. They are not strong team players. They want to be the **team leader.** When they are in leadership positions (assuming they are qualified for the position), they are capable of making massive contributions to the organization fortunate enough to have them. They can be the true **change agents** in organizations. Their energy and focus is enviable to others and many describe them as **role models.** Triangles are **empowering** to others.

Chapter 7

The Triangle at Home

As dominant as the triangle is at work, the same characteristics can emerge in the home setting. We often refer to the triangle as the "executive style." This is the person who needs to be in charge. The dominant personality of the triangle can wreak havoc on the home setting if allowed to run unbridled. If you live with one of these people, this chapter will assist you in putting your situation into perspective. The triangle is not a bad person, he/she merely wants things done the right way—his/her way!

It is important to mention that not all triangles seek dominance in the home environment. Some fill their need for controlling others at work, and become truly passive at home. I have known some triangle people who were roaring lions at the office, and pussycats at home. Apparently, their strong need for control is satisfied at work. The home is a place where they seek quiet submission.

Both situations can be uncomfortable for those who live with triangles. On the one hand, the dominator brings his/her whip home and makes everyone jump! This is most typical. On the other hand, the triangle spouse who is looking for peace and quiet, expects the home to be smooth and worry-free. This person cannot tolerate any problems after 5 P.M., and you had better have dinner ready and pleasant smiles plastered on the faces of family members when the battle-worn triangle walks through the door. Either way, the triangle is in control!

THE TRIANGLE SPOUSE

How to Create an Ideal Triangle Home

1. Take a cue from the box—be **organized**.
2. Establish **routines** for family members.
3. Display **achievements** (awards, grade cards, news articles, trophies,

etc.). Many triangles have trophy cases in their living rooms. Some cover bulletin boards or the refrigerator door with the latest accomplishments.

4. Use **modern decor.** The triangle wants to be "in." Whatever is the latest in home decoration is important. You may be constantly redecorating to stay in fashion.

5. Don't forget the "bells and whistles." Triangles need the latest **electronic gadgets.** They may never figure out how to use them, but they want them displayed prominently in their home.

6. **Status symbols.** You name it. Big house in the "best subdivision," foreign car, monogrammed clothes: the triangle doesn't want to "keep up with the Joneses." The triangle *wants to be the Joneses!*

7. **Spacious interior.** 3,000+ square footage with an "open environment." In America, *big* is power. The home must reflect this ownership of large space.

8. Money is no object. Fortunately, triangles usually make lots of it, so there's no problem. If there is a problem, don't tell your triangle. All the neighbors are in debt too.

9. Join the **best seller** condensed book club. Triangles must be well informed, but want it "quick and dirty." They love reading about successful companies and adore biographies of famous people like Lee Iaccoca or Ted Turner.

10. Give your triangle **unconditional support** (not necessarily love). Families of triangles are expected to make sacrifices. You made your bed, now you must lie in it.

Recreation for the Triangle

1. **Work Hard, Play Hard Philosophy of Life.** Triangles tend to believe in this.

2. **Organized Events.** Since triangles belong to all of the private clubs, civic organizations, and are patrons of the local symphony, there are always requisite events to attend. (Plan a budget that includes money for a tuxedo and dresses by famous-name fashion designers.)

3. **Vast Network of People.** *Note:* I did not say friends. Triangles have many associates and few close friends. Those who are allowed to get close tend to be other triangles and a few circles who give unconditional support.

4. **Famous Friends.** Triangles love to associate with famous people. They tend to have friends who are involved in politics (state and national level preferred). They will often go out of field to associate with local athletes, moguls, and the wealthy.

5. **Competitive Sports.** Triangles love it! They will play any game in

which the winning and losing are clear. Many excel in tennis and racquetball. Whatever the choice, they intend to win.

6. Physical Activity Is Important. If too busy to participate in organized competitive sports, the triangle will develop a personal exercise schedule. They often belong to spas and many have their own home gym.

7. Hands-on Hobbies. Although triangles are not big hobby persons, they do enjoy some yardwork or building activities. They are not fix-it people; they like to start from scratch and create something new.

8. A Popular Form of Recreation for Triangles Is Belonging to Civic Organizations. Often, this is merely an outgrowth of their job. Whether it's Rotary or Boy Scouts, the triangle will become the president within the first five years of membership.

9. Vacations Must Be Active. Triangles cannot stand to lie on the beach all afternoon! They prefer short junkets (weekends) to exotic places. More affluent triangles belong to yacht clubs and travel internationally via Concorde jets.

10. Investment Avocation. Many triangles become heavily involved in investing. They may even develop a second business dealing in stocks, mutual funds, or real estate. Their risk-taking proclivity often pays off here. They are not afraid to use professionals to advise them. Sometimes they own separate businesses as well. When they **retire,** triangles often have a second career already in place.

What to Expect from Your Triangle Spouse

Pluses

1. Quick thinking and decision-making.
2. High energy and fast-paced life.
3. A "can-do" attitude toward problem-solving.
4. Practical, common sense approach.
5. Strong, basically traditional values.
6. Works hard and plays hard, too.
7. Firm commitments to others.
8. Successful!

Minuses

1. Must be **in control** at all times!
2. Inability to admit mistakes.
3. Impulsive with decisions.
4. Temper tantrums; capable of physical violence.
5. Compulsive behavior: may drink/smoke too much.

6. Absent from family activities—or, if present, often distracted. Work is more important.

7. Not openly affectionate in public. Strong showing privately. Triangles must appear self-sufficient.

8. Manipulation. True triangles are not above little white lies when it's necessary to have their way.

Triangles can self-destruct and can destroy everyone in their path at the same time if left to their own devices. Since they do not allow many people to get close to them, you, as the spouse, are one of the rare few. (Even some spouses do not feel close to their triangles!)

If you hope to enhance the relationship between you and your triangular spouse, you can provide a home environment in which the positive qualities of the triangle will blossom and thrive. This will not only make life easier for you and your family, but it will help your triangle in the process. The next two sections will assist you in learning how to live with this strong personality.

How to "Accentuate the Positive" in Your Triangle Spouse

1. **Save Face in Mistakes.** Triangles don't like to be wrong. You might suggest that new data is now available which the triangle didn't have before.

2. **Get the Secretary on Your Side.** She can help you in the personal arena also.

3. **Get Involved in His/Her Business!** Many triangle spouses function as sounding boards.

4. **Be Flexible!** Triangles are impulsive and you must learn to "ride the tide" of change.

5. **Be a Good Listener.** Triangles need to tell people what they think. If you will listen first, the triangle will listen to your ideas later.

How to "Soften" Your Driving Triangle

1. **Plan Quiet "Downtime" Between Hectic Activities.** The triangle will tend to race headlong from one thing to the next. You may need to call a halt on occasion.

2. **Develop an Exercise Schedule.** Triangles tend to be naturally athletic. Participate with your spouse. This may be the only time you are alone together!

3. **Play the Devil's Advocate When Facing a Problem Together.** The triangle has trouble listening to conflicting points of view. This method forces him/her to listen without taking it personally or feeling you are against him/her.

4. Don't Present a Problem Until You Have Thoroughly Analyzed It. If you don't have all your facts straight, the triangle loses respect for you.

5. Learn to be a Referee! Triangles have lots of opponents. You will find yourself in the middle more than once. You may have to save face for both parties.

6. Protect Your Children. Triangles as parents can *push too hard*. They want excellent achievement. If your child can't provide it, you may have to intervene and soften the situation.

7. Offer Multiple Solutions and Ideas to Solve Problems. Triangles tend to lock into one way of doing it. They need someone to provide *creative balance*. Often a squiggle spouse is a good choice for a triangle for this reason.

8. Don't Push Your Triangle into a Corner! He/she will either lie or come out fist first! *Avoid direct competition.* Choose a separate field in which to work if possible.

9. Do Not Tolerate Temper Tantrums! Leave if you must. Ultimately, the triangle does not respect those he/she can push around. Be firm in pointing out that this relationship is a *partnership*, or you'll end up on the short end of the stick for years to come.

10. Develop Inner Strength and Outside Activities for Yourself! Your triangle is self-centered and you must learn to protect yourself to survive. If you wanted a partner who was loving and nurturing, you should have chosen a circle!

Note: These are strong words, but triangles are tough people—as tough on themselves as on others. As the spouse, you can modify and soften this some, but you must also learn to protect yourself. You will take pride in your triangle, but you must also maintain your own self-esteem.

HOW TO FIND A TRIANGLE MATE

Places to Find Triangles

1. In the boardroom, the corner office, the top floor
2. At the home of a prestigious friend
3. At the "in-scene" bars/restaurants
4. At the private club
5. Sitting at the head table at the dinner party
6. Speaking at your professional meeting
7. At Chamber of Commerce coffees/mixers

8. Sitting in first class on the airplane
9. At the political campaign headquarters
10. In professional jobs: medicine, law, etc.
11. At private resorts and on expensive cruises
12. In the private lounge of the bank
13. In the wine cellar
14. In the "smoking area" (if a non-smoker—distributing pamphlets against it)

What to Say to a Triangle

1. "Tell me *all* about yourself!"
2. "What do you think of airline Frequent Flyer programs?"
3. "Do you like to travel—on business or pleasure?"
4. "Do you prefer domestic or imported wines/cars?"
5. "Who is your candidate for senator?"
6. "What is your opinion of the Middle East crisis?"
7. "Did you know JFK personally?"
8. "What a smart suit! Is it Hart, Schaffner, and Marx/Christian Dior? I saw it in *W*."
9. "Seems like I'm always in a hurry. How about you?"
10. Anything witty and slightly gutsy.

What to Do on the First Date

1. Do it all! Pull out all the stops. Make a big splash early with a triangle! Spend lots of dollars on the top flight restaurant/play/social event. Rent a limo and look stupendous!
2. Say little about yourself—just *make an impression.*
3. Wait to call again for at least a week, maybe two.

How to Approach the "Sexual Question"

1. *Don't!* And don't discuss it! The triangle will decide for him/herself! Once the decision is made, be prepared to be *attacked!* (For men, premature ejaculation is not uncommon—don't make it a big deal. He just couldn't wait!)
2. On later dates, demonstrate status through invitations to private parties and events: prestigious dinner parties, private club functions, etc.

3. Always give special attention to proper, fashionable wardrobe and manners. Wear gloves, your Phi Beta Kappa key, and take your opera glasses.

4. Demonstrate appreciation through "special gifts" used to trigger his/her memory of that special evening: engraved crystal, jewelry, etc.

5. If the relationship begins to waiver, take drastic measures. A sure-fire hook for a triangle is the built-in *competition*. Dredge up an old boy/girlfriend. If none are available, hire a wino off the street to pose as the former lover returning to claim his/her prize.

6. **Making the proposal** is very simple with a triangle. Get to the *bottom line*: "Will you or won't you?" Of course if you pop the question with some flair, it helps. Consider proposing on the deck of the cruise ship, on top of the mountain, or at least in the bathtub!

THE TRIANGLE CHILD

It is important to note that triangular children often have certain positioning in the family. They are often the *first child* and also often the *only child* of the parents. As the first child, there is a tendency to feel highly responsible for the younger siblings, plus the fact that first children are often pushed by the parents to succeed. These early messages mold them into triangular personalities.

The only child often becomes a triangle because he/she may tend toward *self-centeredness*. If he/she is bright and quick-witted, the triangle child learns to manipulate his/her environment to meet his/her needs. Parents of only children may indulge them with material goods in order to make up for the lack of siblings. Not needing to share, the child grows up thinking the world is his/her oyster and expects others to acquiesce to his/her needs. Often, parents contribute by instilling *high achievement needs* in their one and only. They expect the only child to be everything they were not.

The firstborn becomes triangular because of over-extended feelings of responsibility. This triangle is often an **overachiever.** The only child behaves as a triangle due to expectations that he/she is "special" and must live up to that in word and deed throughout life. Both situations put *high demands* on their recipients. Thus, many triangles can become **frustrated children** who cannot seem to accomplish the unrealistic goals set for them, or set by them.

This is not necessarily the case, of course. Many triangle children do become highly successful in the world. However, the same negative and positive traits of the triangular adult will manifest themselves in the triangular child. If you have one of these in your life, it will be useful to read this section.

Major Problems/Solutions

Problem 1: Insistence on Having It Their Way. This will manifest itself early in the triangle child. Temper tantrums and parental manipulation make these children tough to deal with.

Solution: This child must learn that he/she cannot live in this world alone and will not always have his/her way. Parents must establish themselves as the boss early. (Note: this is particularly difficult for the circle parent.)

Problem 2: Risk-taker. The triangle child will try anything once! From standing on the seat of the bicycle at age six to driving the family car too fast at 16, the triangle wants to be the leader and can do outrageous things for recognition. Watch out: this can include drugs.

Solution: Regulate the peer group. Channel the child's desire to accomplish into less dangerous areas. Emphasize the importance of good grades for life success. (The triangle can make straight A's if he/she wants to!)

Problem 3: "But Everyone Has One . . . ." This child needs status symbols early. If your money is tight, this can be a major problem, because triangles need to show their importance through material things. They will argue long and skillfully: "But you just got that new set of golf clubs! Why can't I have the dirt bike that I want?"

Solution: Make him/her work for it! Either through outside jobs or jobs around the home for pay, the triangle will do what is necessary to get what he/she wants. This is a child who understands logic (left-brained). You can explain the family budget and the value of work. He/she will understand.

Problem 4: Fear of Failure. This is a really tough one. The triangle wants to be the best at everything. Sometimes this becomes compulsive to the point that this child will avoid things that he/she cannot win immediately and with little effort.

Solution: Allow mistakes early in life. Do not try to create a perfectionist. Create an atmosphere of *exploration* in which many things can be tried, whether they are succeeded at or not.

Problem 5: Lying/Cheating. Sometimes the triangle child's need to be the best gets the better of him/her. When it doesn't seem possible to win, and the triangle still *must* win, he/she may seek unethical means to do so. The triangle is the most prone to *criminal behavior* of the five shapes.

Solution: Build in a strong *value system* of right and wrong early in life. This can also be developed by stressing in your firstborn a sense of responsibility toward others.

Problem 6: Injuries. Because triangles can be "devil may care" in their risk-taking, they often go out on the limb and fall off (literally!). They are athletic by nature, and their overconfidence leads them to attempt physical feats prematurely.

Solution: Expect a few doctor bills along the way. The major injuries will be broken bones, usually nothing very serious. Remember, the triangle is not accident-prone (that's the rectangle).

What to Expect from a Triangle Child at Home

1. Good grades—this is the A student!
2. Opinions . . . . about everything, all the time.
3. Early career choice; try to provide guidance early. Once the triangle decides, it's tough to change it.
4. High personal goals. This person is ambitious. He/she wants to be better than mom and dad.
5. Hero worship. This goes with the goals. It may be a rock star or a pilot, but role models will be important.
6. Posters on the walls. These provide stimulation to the triangle. They will often reflect goals and heroes.
7. Competition. The triangle thrives on it. If there are siblings, the triangle will win.
8. Award collector. Triangles have blue ribbons and trophies all over. This is a good incentive to get this child to clean up his/her room, etc.
9. Argument. Watch out—he/she wants his/her way.
10. Constant activity. From the colicky baby to the "terrible 2s" stage lasting until age 6, the triangle demands *attention* and will get it one way or another.

How to Raise a Triangle Child

1. Be Firm! Avoid a battle of wills. Use punishment when necessary, but be sure the child understands why!

2. Use Rewards. This child responds well to tasks when there's something in it for him/her. A few pennies or a blue ribbon will do it.

3. Give Praise. This is critical to the triangle.

4. Allow Participation in Rule Making. Although you must keep the upper hand, this child is a negotiator and early development of these skills will be useful to him/her.

5. Occasionally Put the Child in Control. When the triangle child is placed in a position of authority, he/she takes it very seriously. This is the child to leave in control of the brothers and sisters.

6. Do Not Stifle Dreams. Although you may feel that some of the child's goals are unattainable, many triangles *do make it*! Don't send early messages like, "Who do you think you are wanting to be a doctor!" He/she may well be one!

7. Save Your Money! Triangle children are expensive! They want the best and are most often *deserving* of it! This child will need college for career fulfillment; some will earn scholarships on their own. Regardless the career choice, the triangle will succeed; for example, the military officer, the executive secretary, the store manager. Mediocre isn't enough.

8. Be Proud! Don't be embarrassed to talk about the accomplishments of this child. This will please him/her and will make him/her try even harder! Luckily, you'll have lots to talk about!

SUMMARY

If there are triangles in your life, you are very fortunate. The spouse will see that you are well provided for. You will bask in the glory of associating with this successful person. Your life will be a constant flow of exciting people and places. Nothing will stay the same; the triangle is a change agent who is always striving for something better.

If the triangle in your life is your child, just try to keep up! This is a real challenge. If you can meet it, the rewards will be abundant, and you will certainly be taken care of in your old age, never fear. This child will be successful.

The downside of all of this is the triangle's need for dominance and control. These are not always pleasant people to live with. Those who live with them often feel dominated and manipulated. You *must* protect yourself in this relationship. You must establish your own turf and insist upon your needs being met also. The triangle will make you subservient if you are not firm.

Although you will take pride in your triangle, you must develop your own *inner strength*. If you will give your triangle your love and support and still maintain your own self-respect and esteem, you will develop a relationship that can be gloriously fulfilling for a lifetime.

Chapter 8

The Triangle at Work

If you work with a triangle, good luck! The triangle wants to do it his/her way. Most triangles want to be the boss—if they aren't already. Of course, these individuals are highly respected in the workplace for their ability to make swift decisions. They are admired for their sureness and the confidence with which they accept responsibility. No other shape is as outwardly self-assured as is the triangle.

Triangles are often found in the following types of jobs:

executive/business owner	union organizer/officer
manager/supervisor	politician
hospital administrator	orchestra conductor
school administrator	entrepreneur
military officer	pilot
law firm partner	

Many triangles hold less prestigious positions: executive secretary, project team leader, staff coordinator, store manager, salesperson. Wherever they are, they try to wield power!

The major characteristics of triangles are that they are suited to leadership, are focused, decisive, ambitious, competitive, athletic, and bottom-line oriented. Because these traits are highly valued in our society, the triangle tends to advance to a position of authority swiftly, in most organizations.

HOW TRIANGLES HANDLE CONFLICT

This section will be particularly important to you if you work with (or for) a triangle. Remember that triangles want it their way, thus, they often use *direct confrontation* when dealing with conflict. Their preferred conflict style is **competition**. However, they are capable of using **compromise** effectively also.

Remember the old saying, "I don't get mad, I get even!" Triangles do both: they get mad *and* they get even! At least, this is true of the classic triangular personality.

This makes them difficult for the other shapes to work with. Although the triangle is familiar with the concept of *team* because of his/her athletic background, he/she wants the rest of us to be the team with the triangle as the *coach*! If the triangle is in a leadership position by title and rank in the organization, no problem. However, if he/she is a peer or a subordinate of yours, this need to be in charge can be highly problematic.

If you are in direct disagreement with a triangle, you may meet with strong resistance in resolving the problem. These people tend to be *dogmatic* about their views. They have a great need to be right and . . . . they have difficulty admitting that they were wrong.

The good news is that you will always know where the triangle stands. He/She will not *avoid* the conflict as boxes often do. There are no secrets. The triangle will be up front with you. Many prefer this method, because there is a minimum of behind-the-back grumbling and subterfuge. These reactions will erode the ability of the workers and finally lead to negative attitudes that impair productivity.

Not so with triangles. The argument will surface quickly and be resolved just as quickly. The only problem is the triangle usually wins! If this happens often enough, co-workers begin to build resentment and the triangle may be isolated from the team.

If you are in conflict with a triangle, the next section will give you some ideas on how to emerge a winner . . . . and how to gain the respect of your fellow triangle at the same time!

HOW TO WIN AN ARGUMENT WITH A TRIANGLE

1. **You Have One Shot Only!** The triangle is a quick decision maker. You've got to make your one shot work!

2. **Be Thoroughly Prepared!** Do extensive research on both your side of the issue *and* the triangle's side. Consider yourself to be a *debator*; a good debator can argue *either side* of the issue with equal ease. This extra effort in preparation will pay off, because the triangle tends to see only one perspective—his/her own.

3. **Present Your Data Logically and Sequentially.** The triangle is a left-brainer. Do not jump from point to point in an erratic fashion. This will give the triangle the advantage since the triangle is skilled at *focusing* directly on the major issue.

4. Maintain Emotional Control! This is critical with triangles because they often lose control. If you can do it, this alone will give you the advantage in the argument.

Note: You will be more capable of maintaining your emotional control if you *rehearse* ahead of time. Know exactly what you are going to say and why. Anticipate the triangle's reactions to your statements and plan your rebuttals. Enlist the aid of your spouse in staging a mock argument with your spouse playing the role of your triangle adversary. This is an excellent method of rehearsal for you.

5. Get an Early "No" from the Triangle. This is a method I learned from a former triangular boss of mine. The triangle wants to tell you *no,* so, in the beginning, ask for agreement on something of *lesser importance* to you and let him/her say no. The logic behind this technique is that this will get it out of his/her system. Once having told you no, the triangle will be more willing to agree to the next (more important) request.

6. When the Triangle Disagrees and It Looks Like You've Lost the Battle, Pull Out the "Ace up Your Sleeve." Always save the clincher until last! Remember, the triangle's "no" can change to "yes" just as quickly.

7. Don't Lock Into Any One Decision. Have several alternative solutions that you can live with. In this way, you assure yourself of walking out a winner regardless the outcome. If the triangle doesn't buy solution A, then agreement on solution C is something you can live with.

8. Wait for a Better Day. Timing is important. This may not be the right time to approach the triangle with this problem. Wait until the triangle is "on a roll" with everything going right for him/her. That's the time he/she can afford to give in and lose one.

9. Prepare to Lose. Although this is not pleasant advice, it is realistic when doing battle with a triangle. But . . . . be a *good loser* and pledge your support for the triangle's final decision. This will pay off in the long run. You must know when to lose the battle to win the war!

10. Finally . . . . Give Some Thought to Telling Other Co-Workers About the Result of the Altercation. Remember how important it is to triangles to be right. If you must continue to work with this triangle—and if you are smart—you will not brag about your win. In fact, the best advice is to *allow the triangle to announce his/her loss.* If you are the loser, then you should tell the others about it first.

THE TRIANGLE CO-WORKER

This is a particularly difficult situation for many of the other shapes, due to the fact that the triangle co-worker is not in a position of authority, but would like to be. Thus, the need to be in charge is not satisfied and the triangle may attempt to control co-workers to satisfy it.

The following is a list of typical problems which people face when working on a peer level with triangles. If this applies to you, the solutions may make your life easier at work.

Problem 1: "I'll Take the Responsibility on This One." This means that the triangle wants you to back off because he/she wants the *credit* for the success of this project.

Solution: Stress the importance of *team effort* on this project. Note major contributions made by others. Show equal strength by pointing out your own willingness to take responsibility as well.

Problem 2: "I don't have time for this . . . . I have important work to do!" What the triangle has to do is more important than what you have to do, of course!

Solution: Demonstrate clearly the ways in which you have taken time out of your busy schedule in the past to assist the triangle! Show willingness to help in the future and call in your chit for past favors you have done. Triangles do understand the chit game of favor for favor. They will play it as long as there is something in it for them.

Problem 3: "Either __ or Get Off the Pot!" Triangles are impatient people. They do not respect others who seem to be *indecisive* and wishy-washy.

Solution: Do not use a triangle as a sounding board. Do your homework and come to the triangle with both problem and solutions well thought out. The triangle will readily give you his/her support if he/she can agree on a clear-cut course of action.

Problem 4: "So Get to the Point!" Triangles are both impatient and bottom-line oriented. They do not appreciate belaboring over all the picky little details (like the box). Nor do they want to chit-chat about it (like the circle).

Solution: "KISS it" (Keep it short and simple) when you present information to a triangle.

Problem 5: "This One Can't Wait . . . . We've Got to Move Fast!" If the triangle had his/her way, this would be true of everything! These people like to shoot from the hip, and they often trod over others in the process. The triangle must be harnessed and must learn to live with the process of systematic accomplishment of the goal. A major triangular flaw is making decisions too quickly without information to support the decision.

Solution: Suggest the triangle attend a training program on planning and coordinating; management systems; or project planning. Although it will bore him/her to death (the program probably is taught by a box), it will teach the principles of systematizing procedures.

Problem 6: "You Can Count on My Support . . . ." This means it is *your baby*, not the triangle's. Why? Because the triangle figures there's nothing in it for him/her. Unless there is something in it for the triangle, he/she will sit the bench and watch.

Solution: Make sure there is something in it for the triangle. If so, you'll get more than support, you'll get active participation and a real advocate for your cause.

Problem 7: "It's Not Good Timing." This is a dead giveaway of the triangle's ability to access the *political* environment. Triangles seem to have a "sixth sense" about the politics of an organization.

Solution: Trust the triangle on this one! He/she is usually right about the politics. Wait and present your case later, and the triangle will lend his/her support. It's a good idea to test the political waters with a triangle first to be sure your proposal will fall on receptive ears.

Problem 8: "It's Your Move!" The triangle is testing you. The world is a big chess game, and it's your turn to demonstrate your ability. This means the triangle feels that he/she has the upper hand in the situation.

Solution: Make your move, but make it when you are ready. Don't let the triangle control you.

Problem 9: "I Need a Favor." This is said usually after the triangle has hurriedly entered your office and closed the door behind him/her.

Solution: Be cautious. Listen to the proposal carefully. This could be a trap: an attempt to pass a "hot potato" to you. If you decide to grant the favor, be very sure to end the discussion with four simple words . . . . "You owe me one!" Triangles understand the trade-off game and are experts at playing it.

Triangles are really not so hard to work with if only you know how to deal with them. If you don't, they can dominate you and maneuver you into corners before you know it. A bit of healthy suspicion is good when working with a triangle. Remember, the triangle is looking out for "numero uno"!

THE TRIANGLE BOSS

This section is very important to every reader because more bosses act like triangles than any other shape. Please observe that I said *act like*, not that more bosses *are* triangles. *American attitudes toward leadership reinforce triangular behavior in people who hold positions of authority.* Whether the boss is a triangle or not, he/she will surely demonstrate the characteristics whenever possible. How skillfully he/she does so will reveal whether or not he/she is a true triangle.

There are two shapes which tend to *masquerade as triangles* when they are in leadership positions: the rectangle and the box! The rectangle is the person in a state of transition. He/she moves erratically from taking a hard line position to total avoidance of the whole situation. This person is unsure of how to behave and will act like a triangle one day and be a circle or a squiggle the next.

The most typical imitator of the triangle is a box in a position of authority. In fact, many *boxes actually believe that they are triangles*! The true box will eventually be discovered, however. The box nature will emerge under crisis. Instead of reacting swiftly to resolve the problem as a triangle does, the box will drag his/her feet and procrastinate, hoping it will all go away or resolve itself. Boxes also differ from triangles in that they are much more *detail-oriented* and insist on putting it in writing. Triangles prefer crisis management and have an aversion toward paperwork in general. The box is also a better team-player than the triangle who wants credit.

What to Expect from Your Triangle Boss

Pluses

1. Commitment to excellence
2. Work hard/play hard philosophy
3. Rolled-up sleeves right along with you
4. Political expertise (your department will be in a "fishbowl" constantly)
5. Clear direction
6. Firm decisions
7. Great in a crisis!
8. Will give you a second chance—but no third!

Minuses

1. Long hours; triangles work 7 A.M. to 7 P.M.
2. Zero errors; they don't tolerate mistakes.
3. "Look good" philosophy (seems more important to look good than to do it right!)
4. Difficulty admitting mistakes
5. Delegates . . . . but takes the credit
6. "Hip-shooter" decisions
7. Hard to please; tough on self and others.
8. No downtime . . . . expects 150 percent all the time . . . . both at work and play. This is the *driver* personality.

How to Please Your Triangle Boss

1. Do your job! And do it well.
2. Do the "little extras": work late and make it clear you had to cancel dinner (sacrifice).
3. Show leadership within your team.
4. Show leadership outside also; i.e., President of Kiwanis, American Business Women's Association.
5. *Always* share the credit with the boss.
6. Keep boss informed on a timely basis. (Triangles hate to hear the bad news elsewhere!).
7. Never *end-run* a triangle (do not go over his/her head to the big boss).
8. Don't "badmouth" the team.
9. Demonstrate your ability to handle yourself with ease and expertise at *social events*. (This is important at the higher levels and this demonstrates your political savvy.)
10. Make all communications direct and succinct, both written and face-to-face.

A final piece of advice when working for a triangle boss: Capitalize on the *"he thinks like we do"* philosophy. This is the traditional way to get promoted by triangles. Because triangles have such a healthy respect for their own abilities, they also admire others who act and think like they do. These are the ones whom they will reward. Be sure you are one.

THE TRIANGLE CUSTOMER

How to Identify the Triangle Customer

1. **Expensive clothing** worn in a casual way
2. **Smooth body movement;** looks like he/she has been here before
3. **Piercing eye contact**
4. **Firm handshake**
5. Questions appear **casual,** like afterthoughts
6. Some brief small talk, quick wit and rapport
7. Fast assessment of a situation; eyes dart quickly over your product display
8. Appears **relaxed** but indicates time pressure

9. Wants to be **told** about product/service; unwilling to spend time reading materials
10. Strong sense of **power** and **class**; many mediocre salespersons are simply overpowered by triangle customers

How to "Sell" the Triangle Customer

1. Be prepared to negotiate; the triangle doesn't accept the first offer. Even if the price is not negotiable, the triangle will try to get the installation free.
2. Talk fast. Triangles are busy people.
3. Get to the bottom line (only the major details).
4. Stress the main features, but mention at least one negative quality. The triangle respects people who are up front with him/her.
5. Answer questions honestly and don't underestimate the knowledge of this customer.
6. Totally focus on the triangle; drop everything else. The triangle must have your complete attention.
7. Talk status . . . . drop names of other customers who have purchased your product.
8. Demonstrate your own track record. Triangles like to know that they are dealing with successful people.
9. Expect some limited comparison shopping. You probably have one major competitor for the triangle's business. Find out who it is and outsell them.
10. Ask for the sale directly—and early. The triangle respects courage and risk-taking. He/she may make an impulsive decision and buy on the spot. Of course, if it was a bad decision expect the triangle to return it just as fast.

Final note: Triangles have no loyalty to any one company or manufacturer. They go for the best quality and the best deal. However, they are prone to impulse buying and they tend to prefer "name brands." You may be able to capitalize on these characteristics of the triangle customer.

SUMMARY

Whether you are a salesperson in the throes of trying to sell a triangle customer, or a subordinate trying to please a triangle box, the situation is the same. The triangle wants to **win** the advantage for him/herself. As long as you are armed with this knowledge, you can counteract the **strong force** of the triangular personality.

You can expect the triangles with whom you work to be **outspoken** and **confident.** You will find them to be **courageous** (intrepid) in their desire to make an impact on the world. The triangle is the **risk-taker** among us. If he/she chooses the right situation in which to take the risk, he/she is bound to win big. You can hold onto the coattails of a triangle, and the ride will be fast and sure—directly vertical. (Note: triangles can fall downward just as dramatically as they ascended!) Luckily, the true triangle (not the box imitator) has the skills to get to the top and to stay there!

Triangles tend not to **trust** many people, particularly work associates. This protects them against forming emotional liaisons which they may have to **betray** to get ahead later. Nothing and no one is more important than the triangle's career. So, beware and learn to protect yourself. As **admired** and **emulated** as triangles are by others, they can be deadly if you cross them. The best advice is to admire from afar!

Chapter 9

_____ The Triangle Under Stress

It seems strange to devote a chapter to this subject because, of all five shapes, the triangle is most likely to live a stressful life *by choice*! Triangles tend to be their own worst enemies when it comes to applying pressure. Many triangles report that they are happiest when they have deadlines to meet and tension in their lives. People who work for triangles report that their triangle boss is most disturbed when things are going smoothly in the office! They say the boss is at his/her best when there is a crisis!

Of course, this is all consistent with the personality of the triangle. They are action-oriented. They like to be in control and enjoy making the decisions necessary to resolve the crisis situation. They tend to **manage by crisis.** This is true both at work and at home.

We all need a certain amount of tension in our lives to function effectively. If not enough is happening, we get bored and listless, and life just isn't exciting and challenging enough. However, if too much is going on, we feel stressed out and unable to cope. Each person has his or her own "tolerance point" at which he/she can't take anymore.

However, some people can tolerate much more activity and confusion than others; their tolerance level is much higher. These people will even seek to increase the activity in their lives. In psychological studies, they are called the *stimulation seekers* or "Type A" personalities. These are the triangles among us. What would drive a box to drink is a quiet day for a triangle!

Keep this in mind, then, as you read this chapter about the triangles in your life. They tend to experience stress in two different circumstances: (1) when there is not enough going on, and (2) when there is *too* much going on. The first situation is often not controlled by them. The second is usually a direct result of the triangle's own tendency to take on too much.

When the triangle *loses control*, it is devastating! In this way, the triangle is, indeed, his/her own worst enemy.

How to Identify a Triangle Under Stress

1. **Frenetic Activity.** Because the triangle is such a focused person, when the going gets tough, the triangle gets even tougher! He/she devotes body and soul to the tasks (always more than one) at hand! Efforts are doubled both at work and play.

2. **Fury.** When the triangle has indeed bitten off more than he/she can chew, rather than retreat, he/she will express anger towards others. This is when you need to get out of his/her way!

3. **Disheveled Appearance.** Triangles work hard at looking relaxed and "in control." When they don't, you know something is wrong.

4. **Habit Intensification.** If your triangle is a smoker or a drinker, he/she may become *compulsive* about the habit during the stressful period. Everything speeds up on high.

5. **Hypercritical of Everything** . . . . and everyone. You can't please a triangle under stress, no matter how hard you try.

6. **Jerky Body Movements.** This is highly unusual for a triangle who moves smoothly from one situation to the next.

7. **Impatience.** It just can't be done soon enough. "I need it yesterday," says the triangle.

8. **Swearing.** Male triangles will begin to sound like drunken sailors during this period. Female triangles may either emulate the men or *cry* a lot. This is the devastation a triangle feels when he/she begins to lose control.

9. **Frequent Colds/Flu.** Of course, the body reacts synchronically. We are all most susceptible to illness during times of stress.

10. **Avoidance of Friends/Family.** This is a very harmful behavior, because during stressful times, we need our "support system" the most! Triangles will avoid those who know them well as a result of their pride. They don't want others to see that they are over their heads because they are fearful of losing their respect.

Sources of Stress for Triangles

It is important to point out that the major source of stress for the triangle is work. This is only true of triangles. The other four shapes experience more serious stress from problems in their personal lives than they do from work-related problems. This is not so with the triangle! Although a triangle does need people to recognize his/her ability and achievements, a smooth homelife is not as crucial to him/her as it is to the other shapes. Triangles are the most capable of living alone of the five shapes. For this reason, the *major sources of stress are work-related for triangles*:

1. **One Crisis Too Many!** Loss of control is the number one problem here. Triangles have to be in control of their life circumstances. Those who lose control often revert to a *rectangular* period that is painful in their lives.

2. **Loss of Sense of Direction.** This is very debilitating to a triangle. The focus must be clear at all times.

3. **Loss of Status/Demotion.** When this happens, the triangle will try to gain status another way.

4. **Failure.** Although the triangle is capable of taking this in stride, he/she works hard to prevent it.

5. **Unqualified Employees.** If the triangle is the boss (highly likely) and the subordinates or co-workers are not equipped to do the job, it is very frustrating to him/her.

6. **Change in the Rules.** This is fine if it is the triangle's decision. However, if *new leadership* comes in (such as a corporate take-over), the resulting chaos can be highly threatening to the triangle.

7. **No-Win Situation.** Triangles need to win. When they find themselves in a "Catch 22," they're in trouble. (Luckily this doesn't happen often since they are skilled political players.)

8. **Wrong Job.** The wrong job for a triangle is in a *maintenance organization*. This is an organization that is slow to change and merely exists to maintain the ways things have been done in the past; e.g., the government. Boxes work best in this setting. Triangles need more action.

9. **"Dirty Work" Job.** Although triangles are good trouble-shooters and are often moved around from department to department to clean it up, they secretly yearn for their own unit in which they can establish permanent dominance.

10. **Vacation.** These are not pleasant for triangles. Lying on the beach or in a deck chair in the sun all afternoon is totally *boring* for this person. As in every other arena of the triangle's life, action is where it's at. If the triangle does agree to tear him/herself away from the job for a few days, his/her preference is a trip to the mountains with the ski club; a weekend of sailing; a wild party that lasts for several days; or a quick junket to Las Vegas (triangles are often heavy gamblers).

Stressful People for Triangles

Like all of us, there are a few types who tend to get on a triangle's nerves. However, even these people are tolerable to triangles *if* the triangle is in an authoritative position. Stressful people to triangles are squiggles, rectangles, and circles—in that order.

1. **Squiggles.** As you will learn in Section Five, the squiggle is the

least *focused* and *organized* of the five shapes. Squiggles flit from one thing to the next, and this is what drives triangles crazy! Triangles are the most focused of the left-brained shapes, while squiggles are the least focused of the right-brained shapes.

There is one other point of contention between the squiggle person and the triangle. The latter is the most dominant personality of the five shapes. However, the squiggle can be the triangle's equal in personal power when one thing is true: when the squiggle's *idea* is at stake. The squiggle is an idea person. If the triangle disagrees with the squiggle's idea, the sparks will fly! And it's a close contest! Luck is on the side of the triangle, however, since squiggle's will give up first! The triangle can wait out any other shape when winning is at stake.

2. Rectangles. There is both good and bad news here. The rectangle causes problems for the triangle because this person is so *unsure* of him/herself. Triangles do not respect people who are wishy-washy.

The good news is that triangles love to lead others and the rectangle is a prime candidate. This person is highly susceptible to being swayed by a more powerful personality such as the triangle. Once the triangle sees that he/she can *manipulate* the rectangle, then the stress is alleviated. The balance of power is corrected. The triangle is back in control.

3. Circles. The "secret weapon" of many triangles is the circle in their lives. This is often the long-suffering wife/husband who has sacrificed his/her own needs to the more powerful other. However, triangles can develop stress over this situation if they are made to feel *guilty* about it ("Remember who put you through college!") Of course, the circle *chose* the supportive role).

Another aspect of triangle/circle conflict occurs in the work setting. Circles tend to socialize at work and triangles are highly task-oriented instead. They often accuse circles of being over-personal and not serious enough about their jobs. It is triangles who complain about circles taking long lunch hours and making personal phone calls at work. If the triangle is the boss, he/she can put a stop to this and make the circle's life miserable in the process. The two merely have different objectives at work.

HOW THE TRIANGLE DEALS WITH STRESS

Stage 1—Avoidance

1. Refuses to Recognize It! Typical of the "Type A" personality, the triangle is the one who keels over the desk at work of a heart attack. This person pushes him/herself to the limit every day and tends to ignore some of the early warning signs the body sends.

2. Blames Others. When things begin to go awry, it is most characteristic of triangles to become critical of others and to place blame elsewhere.

3. Increases Pace. If it's not working right, the triangle tries to do more of it! He/she will work at a feverish pitch during the early stages of stress.

4. Blames Fatigue. Since triangles already push their bodies to the limit, when things go wrong, they blame their body. Often there is real fatigue due to the fast pace.

5. Social Withdrawal. Under favorable conditions, the triangle likes to have a good time as well as the next person. However, under undue pressure, the social life is the first to go. Work is always more important.

Stage 2—Recognition

Once the triangle is willing to *admit* that he/she is experiencing stress, there are predictable ways that this individual will deal with it. Unfortunately, it is sometimes too late. The triangle may have already experienced a heart attack, lost a job, or alienated friends and/or family.

1. Stringent Exercise. This is the first impulse of the triangle person, and . . . . it's a good one. One of the solutions to stress-related problems is increased exercise. However, the triangle must be cautioned not to overdo it.

2. Executive "Stress Test." This is one of the most useful devices in the medical profession. Many companies have their executives and middle managers go through it regularly. This will pinpoint physical problems resulting from stress quickly.

3. Doctor's Orders. The triangle knows to use experts in solving problems for which he/she is not qualified (CPA's, attorneys, etc.). Thus, when the stress is recognized, he/she will seek medical advice and will adhere to it—at least for awhile.

4. Premature Wellness. Unfortunately, too often the triangle has an unrealistic impression of his/her abilities. Triangles have been known to go back to work a few days after major surgery, etc. They must discipline themselves to go through the recuperation period properly.

How to Help Your Triangle to Reduce Stress

1. Just as You Would with Your Child, Insist upon a Balanced Diet and Plenty of Sleep. Triangles tend to skip lunch and eat heavy dinners, and they can go without sleep more than any of the other shapes.

2. Watch for the Early Warning Signs—the behaviors listed at the beginning of the chapter. One sign alone is no problem. Two or three together can spell trouble.

3. Develop "Calming Cues." I have often seen wives do this with driven executive husbands. These are the taps on the elbow, the subtle raised eyebrow, clearing of the throat, or a simple whispered word. Cues that alert the triangle to calm down.

4. Use Humor! This is one of the best methods, because the triangle is quick-witted and will appreciate it. A little humor goes a long way to diffuse a tense situation for everyone.

5. Change of Scenery. Just getting away—even for a short weekend—will often "soothe the savage beast."

6. Exposure to Old Friends. It is sometimes useful to go back to earlier times when life was not so hectic! Reunions often do this for people.

7. Redirect the Energy. Suggest that your triangle become involved in some new project, perhaps outside the work environment. Something like the United Way, Big Brothers/Sisters, etc. will take his/her mind off of the job.

8. Skillful Spouses and Friends Have Been Known to Take Their Harried Triangle to a Movie or Play about an Overachiever Who Experienced a Terrible Failure. Movies like *Wall Street* or *Broadcast News* come to mind. Of course, literature is full of the tales of overachieving triangles, from *The Caine Mutiny* to *Macbeth* and *Scrooge*. We can often learn about ourselves through the problems of others.

9. Send Your Triangle to a Management Retreat. There are many excellent ones available. Some are even titled "Stress Management." There are also books and tapes available.

10. Teach Your Triangle to Trust Others. This is difficult for triangles, because they want to be self-sufficient. However, we all have some dependence upon other people. During this stressful period, the triangle needs people to talk to and to help him/her. He/she must learn to rely on others now and in the future.

Triangles Feel Most Comfortable When . . . .

1. They are **in control** of the situation.
2. They are the undisputed **authority/leader** of the group.
3. Others are **dependent** upon them.
4. They are in the middle of a **crisis** that they know they can resolve.
5. They are in the position to **write the rules.**
6. They are **heading** a "start-up" or a "clean-up" operation.
7. Their **opinion** is sought by important others.
8. They are a member of a **prestigious group.**
9. They have just won an **award** or some form of personal recognition.

10. They enjoy the **respect** of superiors, peers, and (selected) subordinates.

Final Note

Like boxes, triangles place the greatest emphasis on accomplishing the tasks required in the workplace. Unlike the box, the triangle wants to be "in charge" of those tasks. Being a **hard driver,** the triangle doesn't know when (or how) to slow down, and the debilitating effects of stress often creep in before they are recognized.

If you are a triangle, try to be more aware of the early warning signs that accompany stress. If you are in the position of being a "support person" for a triangle, you can assist your triangle in this process. Encourage him/ her to **slow down** and learn to relax. This is very difficult for the classic triangle, who **works and plays hard.** Triangles must learn to **listen, relax, and rely on others** for their own good.

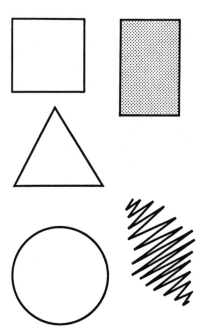

Section Three

THE ERRATIC RECTANGLE

Chapter 10

Identifying the Rectangle . . . . _____ Pick a Card, Any Card

Belief: "There is a pot of gold at the end of the rainbow . . . . I just know it."

Translation: There are better things in life, if only I could discover what they are and how to get them."

You rectangles *know who you are*! You will find nothing I say on the next few pages to be surprising. In fact, most people who discover that they are rectangles are delighted to know it! They have long wondered why they seemed to feel so strange . . . . so unconnected . . . . so unlike themselves. Identifying yourself as a rectangle will help explain this **change** you are going through. As a rectangle, you will learn more from reading this section than any one of the other four shapes, and, in many ways, you need this guidance the most of all. Read on and enjoy!

OVERVIEW

State of Transition defines the situation in which rectangles find themselves. There is movement within the rectangle that is heralding a major **change**. This person's equilibrium is off-balance. There is a sense of incredible **excitement** with each new day. At the same time, however, there is a great deal of **confusion** as well. The change taking place may be personal or professional or both!

Most characteristic of rectangles is their **inconsistent** and **unpredictable** behavior during this period. These are people who are **searching** and **growing.**

They are discovering new ways of living and working. They are trying new things. For this reason, if you must depend on a rectangle, good luck! He/she is highly **changeable** from day to day. In fact, if you look closely, you will notice *behaviors of the other four shapes* within the rectangle. The rectangle wants to be something better, thus, he/she suffers from **low self-esteem** during this time.

Two of the most endearing characteristics of this transitional period in the life of the rectangle are his/her newfound tendency to be **courageous** and **inquisitive**. Rectangles will try things they've never done before! They will ask questions that they lacked the courage to ask before. In fact, during this period, the rectangle is **open, suggestible,** and can be easily **manipulated.** Rectangles must guard against this.

QUICK INDICATORS OF RECTANGLE PEOPLE

Language

Common Words: unsure, explain, wait, analyze, maybe, consider, alternatives, options, why?

Common Sayings: "I . . . . think so!?" "What do *you* think about it?" "I just can't decide?" "I just learned a great new way to do it!" "Why do we do it this way?" "Is this important? Should I take notes?"

Appearance

Men and Women: Erratic and unpredictable appearance. Will wear the three-piece business suit one day and appear in shirt sleeves or mini-skirt the next. Men often develop facial hair during this period; a new mustache appears out of the blue. Women may change their hairstyles entirely. Being a linear shape, the rectangle can plan his/her changes. The rectangle may go on a shopping spree and completely change his/her wardrobe overnight. To others, this may seem silly, but the rectangle is following a master plan.

It is impossible to predict how the rectangle will appear because he/she is in an unfrozen state, in other words, not yet solidified into one of the four *primary states* of the other four shapes. (I once knew a rectangle woman who put on two different shoes from two different pairs and came to work!) I have also noticed that rectangle men seem to have many *hats*. This is symbolic, because in a figurative sense, they "change hats" daily!

Office

There will be strong evidence of the internal *conflict* that the rectangle is feeling. The computer may be found in the middle of a garden of live plants. The family pictures may have fallen behind the desk. Out-basket papers may be put in the in-basket on certain days. Important memos may be found by the janitor in the trash basket. Often, personal effects are lying out in full view: yesterday's lunch on the filing cabinet or dirty clothes to be taken to the cleaners thrown behind the door. There may be four or five umbrellas in the room. Each day a new one is brought in case it rains. There will be a mixture of writing implements on the desk—pens, pencils, markers, etc. The rectangle may take great pride in having his/her *first private office*. He/she may start decorating with an attempt to imitate the triangle boss above him/her. However, since the box is still a strong influence on the rectangle, the confusion will manifest itself in symbols of both of the other shapes.

Personal Habits

1. **Forgetful.** Rectangles often misplace things or forget to bring the important papers to the meeting. This is because there are so many things happening, it's hard to keep track of them all.

2. **Nervous.** Often on-edge because he/she is unsure of the appropriate behavior in the situation.

3. **Late or Very Early.** Again, erratic behavior.

4. **Compulsive.** May overeat, smoke or drink excessively during this period.

5. **Emotional Outbursts.** These are often followed by days of total withdrawal from everyone.

6. **Packrat.** Since the rectangle doesn't know what he/she will need when, it is all kept. This person never throws anything away—purposefully.

7. **Avoids Anything That Smacks of Conflict.** Getting involved might show how unsure he/she is. It's better to stay out of it and let others who know more solve the problems.

8. **Variety.** Constant small changes in behavior of all sorts. For example, he/she may take up smoking one day and drop it in revulsive the next. Be ready for a roller coaster ride if you work with or for a rectangle.

9. **Large Groups.** Rectangles prefer large rather than small groups of people, because they think they can *hide* in the large group. They often avoid one-to-one interaction, for fear of being put on the spot and not knowing what they are expected to know.

10. Blurting Out. The person who has sat quietly throughout the meeting and suddenly blurts out an idea is probably a rectangle. The timing is off.

Body Language

1. Clumsy. This person is not "together" and it shows. He/she may trip or run into a door.
2. Jerky body movements. There may be a strange eye twitch or an arm that seems to move independently from the body. Head movements may be jerky.
3. Nervous habits. Clearing of throat, drumming table, tapping pencils, stroking face, or scratching is common.
4. Flushed face/watery eyes.
5. Fleeting eye contact. Trying to absorb everything, the rectangle flits from one to another, never really pausing anywhere. This is very distracting to others who need his/her attention.
6. High-pitched voice. This is evidence of insecurity—particularly if it is also squeaky.
7. Nervous giggle/laugh.
8. Erratic speech patterns—sudden alteration of volume and/or speed of speech.
9. Unpredictable changes from silence to total animation in body and voice.
10. Note: Read the body language indicators for the other four shapes. *Rectangles may act like any other shape at any time.* As a linear, the box or triangle are the first choices, but rectangles can be circles or squiggles also!

Final Note

You, the rectangle among us, are experiencing a major change in your life. It is exciting, confusing, and altogether an unusual experience for you. Others may look at you as if you are crazy, but don't let this disturb you. We have all passed through periods of change like this and so will you!

It will be beneficial to those around you if you explain to the best of your ability the change you are experiencing. This will help them to understand your inconsistent and unpredictable behavior during this time. They may not like it, but if you will stand firm, they will have to accept it.

Do not let this life change throw you completely off kilter. As we climb the mountain of life, it is easy to stop and rest at the next plateau.

Some people never leave the lower level plateaus at all. However, in order to reach the next plateau, you must get up and climb again. This is the normal progression we humans experience when we grow. You have chosen to climb to a new height . . . . good for you! Keep up the good work and don't turn back. You won't know how beautiful the view is until you reach the top!

Chapter 11

The Rectangle at Home

The most critical element for the rectangle is a very **stable home environment.** Because the rectangle is going through an emotional upheaval, this is the one place in his/her life that *must* be stabilizing. Remember, this is a transitional *stage*; it won't last forever. However, during it, those of you who live with rectangles must make an "extra effort" to adjust.

This all will be much easier if the home situation has been consistent for some time. The more years of experience members of the family have with the rectangle, the better able to cope with his/her change they will be. However, the change also will be a *shock* to family members, particularly to children. Where dad/mom used to be so sure and so predictable, now it seems like he/she has gone off the deep end! Kids will tend to *worry about the rectangle parent*. They must be reassured often and enlisted to help the struggling parent through this period.

There are several "life stages" in which rectangular characteristics are prone to emerge: **new marriage, first baby, divorce, mid-life crisis, new job, retirement, loss of a loved one.** Each of these situations tends to force people into a confused state. It is a time of change and adaptation to a new set of circumstances. This chapter will lend some guidance.

THE RECTANGLE SPOUSE

How to Create an Ideal Rectangle Home

1. Simplify! Do not clutter your rectangle's already spinning mind with more choices. *You must make the decisions now*, more than ever before!
2. Light, Airy Decor. Something in pastels with no more than two or three colors at most. This environment is free of pressure. Dark colors can

be cave-like depressing, while bright colors are over-stimulating to the rectangle. I would also suggest the use of *glass* in linear formations. Remember, the rectangle is a linear shape.

3. Establish Definite Routines. There should be no room for indecision. Hopefully, this will already be true in your home, so that no "new" rules will need to be set in place during the transition period.

4. Simple Meals with Basic Menus Incorporating the Rectangle's Favorite Foods Are Advisable. However, a fully stocked refrigerator for "midnight snacks" is also good.

5. Be Sure to Adhere to Strict Budgeting During This Period. It is best that you control the checkbook, since your spouse may run out and buy unnecessary things to solve his/her problems.

6. A Full Medicine Cabinet Is a Good Idea. Rectangles tend to be *accident prone* during this period. Many will also suffer tension headaches, among other ailments.

7. A Few Little Surprise Gifts. This would be a nice touch to keep spirits up and let your spouse know you care.

8. Patience Is a Critical Virtue During This Transitional Time. All those around the rectangle must do their utmost to show understanding and support. Remember, this, too, shall pass!

Recreation for the Rectangle

1. Lunch Is a Good Break for the Rectangle at Work. Plan to join him/her once a week. This shows your support and gives your spouse a breather. Of course, he/she will have trouble deciding what to order (probably the "combination plate" is the best idea).

2. Avoid Making a Heavy Investment in an Expensive Hobby During This Period. Purchasing a big speedboat with full regalia which may be rejected later is a bad investment.

3. Plan Lots of Social Get-togethers Now. But be prepared for your rectangle to prefer **new friends** to old ones. The reason is simple: he/she is not him/herself now and senses that old friends will find him/her out. However, if old friends are properly prepared, they can be of enormous help and support during this time.

4. This Is a Good Time for a Long Vacation! Choose a calm and relaxing place, since your rectangle needs quiet time for reflection and stabilization.

5. Encourage Participation in Low Exertion Sports. Your rectangle needs exercise, but a mild game of tennis or golf will suffice. Table games with friends are very good.

6. Seek New Recreational Outlets. Do things that the both of you don't often do. Go to the symphony, a play, on a cruise, something new.

The rectangle is testing him/herself, and this provides another outlet to do so.

    7. Anticipate "Last Minute" Changes. Rectangles change their minds at a moment's notice. Have a **contingency plan** in your back pocket.

    8. This Is a Great Time to Go Back to School! Encourage your rectangle to take a course or two. The rectangle is most open to new learning during this stage and will anxiously absorb new ideas. He/she will excel in an academic program now.

    9. Be Sure That Your Rectangle Gets Enough Sleep During This Period. Some rectangles suffer from insomnia, and this merely makes matters worse.

    10. Keep It Light! Whatever you do, don't lose your **sense of humor.** It is critical now! Many rectangles become so dissatisfied with themselves that they complain and grumble and forget to look on the light side. You must help out!

What to Expect from Your Rectangle Spouse

Pluses

1. Excitement! There is never a dull moment.
2. Experimentation. Rectangles want to try new things, because they are testing themselves on all levels.
3. Sudden, unpredictable spurts of energy.
4. Humor. Rectangles who can laugh about their confusion are OK!
5. Playfulness. This is a time for teasing and play-acting. Expect it. Enjoy it.
6. Surprises. Some will be good, some bad.
7. Questions about everything.
8. Unusual caring, empathy, and support for you. Like all of us, rectangles will *give* what they *need*!

Minuses

1. Confusion. Be kind . . . . call it misunderstanding.
2. Erratic, "last minute" changes.
3. Fatigue/minor illness. They are accident prone.
4. Mood swings.
5. Criticism of others. Dissatisfaction with self is transferred to others.
6. Loss of interest or short attention span.
7. Forgetfulness. Too many things are going on. Be forgiving, it isn't intentional.

8. Preoccupation with self. Rectangles may not hear people talking to them. They are lost in their own heads.

How to "Accentuate the Positive" in Your Rectangle Spouse

1. Long Talks. If you can persuade your rectangle to talk about it, good for you—and for him/her!

2. Give Space . . . . lots of it. Try not to make too many demands now.

3. Maintain Old Routines. This is not the time for major changes at home. Something must remain stable.

4. Be Reactionary. What I mean by this is be ready for anything! Do not build expectations of how things should be or how things used to be.

5. Remind Your Rectangle of Past Accomplishments. Some rectangles really get down on themselves. It's good to remind them that they have been successful in the past.

6. Intensify Your Love and Support. Try not to be too critical, even of obvious mistakes.

7. Maintain Your Own Sense of Humor. Although it may be tough to do, it's vital for you and your rectangle.

8. Learn About Stress! It is highly predictable that people in rectangular periods are experiencing stress. Read Chapter Thirteen at the end of this section very carefully. It will have some useful hints for you about helping your rectangle cope with the changes happening within him/her.

HOW TO FIND A RECTANGLE MATE

I must say that it is difficult to understand exactly *why you would want to*, but, if you do, you are probably a rectangle yourself and want company. You even may be a circle seeking someone to help, or a triangle seeking someone to control. Perhaps, you have already found someone who is a rectangle and want to understand him/her. This section will help.

Places to Find Rectangles

1. Singles bars. (Rectangles are often newly unattached.)
2. On the subway in the middle of the night.
3. At the hotel bar in mid-afternoon.
4. In the community college night course.
5. At a public seminar sitting in the last row.

6. At church, hoping the divine spirit will help.
7. In the last row of the airplane (a nonsmoker).
8. At the movies, to take his/her mind off the problems.
9. At home alone.

What to Say to a Rectangle

1. "Tell me about yourself." This allows the rectangle to be anybody he/she wants to be at the moment.
2. "So what do you want to be when you grow up?" This allows unconditional fantasizing.
3. "Let's do . . . ." You decide and force compliance.

What to Do on the First Date

1. Go to a movie/play. This is an escape mechanism.
2. Attend a large party where the rectangle can be anonymous.
3. Play "charades" or *Pictionary*; some game that allows for role-playing and is low risk.
4. Attend a lecture.
5. Attend a sporting event where attention is directed outside of self and no conversation is required.

How to Approach the "Sexual Question"

1. Don't talk about it; rectangles are already confused.
2. Make a firm overture early!
3. Mix with others on the first few dates, then plan a private event. An intimate dinner at your beach condo will do. Waste no time in making your intentions clear. The rectangle is vulnerable and often an "easy mark." Plus, this person *needs affection* now.
4. Regardless of the outcome, continue to give the rectangle your support. This person is going through a tough time and doesn't need to be abandoned—even by a casual acquaintance!

Warning: Rectangles can be taken advantage of during this period of their lives. If you really *care* about your rectangle, slow down. Don't push after the first sexual encounter. Allow the rectangle to make the next move. This is certainly not a good time to suggest marriage! Allow the rectangle to pass through this transition and see what comes out on the other side; then make a long-term decision, not before.

THE RECTANGLE CHILD

It must be pointed out that the rectangular child is merely a child going through a *problem period* in his/her life. If your child has *always* been a problem, if he/she has always been confused and erratic; then, reading this chapter will not help you. You and your child need to seek serious *professional help*!

However, this is unlikely in the majority of cases. In fact, your child is probably completely normal and simply experiencing a problem period in his/her life. Sometimes it seems that the entire childhood period is problematic! This is the stormy time when sudden growth spurts (both physical and psychological) are to be expected. They are the norm! There are many *transitions* to pass through prior to reaching adulthood. We have all experienced them. Your child will pass through several predictable *stages* before he/she can truly be called an adult.

Assuming that you have a *normal child*, the next section will address the normal rectangle periods that he/she must experience and how you might handle them. If you want more information about these predictable, difficult times, a good book on child development is advised.

Problem Periods/Solutions

Problem 1: New School. Whether it's entering school for the *first time* (kindergarten/first grade), graduating from elementary to junior high school, or moving to a new school, it's a tough adjustment for any child!

Solution: Ease the transition by visiting the school early and meeting some of the teachers, if possible. Visit the classroom (if elementary) to assist the child in adjusting. Try to get your child acquainted with classmates in the neighborhood and arrange for him/her to go with them on the first day of school.

Problem 2: Adolescence. This is the big one! Very few children pass through this rectangular period unscathed! This is when your adoring child suddenly has no respect for you or anyone else anymore! It comes earlier for girls (11 to 14) and later for boys (13 through 16). All of the characteristics of the rectangle will emerge during this time. Be ready!

Solution: Think of adolescence as "temporary insanity." This is not your child acting this way! It is, but it isn't. It *is* your child, but he/she is exploring other selves within him/her. This is truly a period of self-searching.

The most important thing you can do is to continue to *show affection*! I mean physical affection. Although the last thing you may feel like doing is hugging the little "monster," that is what he/she needs most from you now!

It is also important to carefully *monitor friends* during this time. Because the child is vulnerable, he/she may be more easily swayed to get involved with the "wrong crowd" doing the wrong things. You may need to be *firm* (yet loving) in controlling the peer relationships.

Problem 3: Moving to a new town, location. This requires upsetting the familiar; finding new school and friends.

Solution: Family togetherness is critical. Until replacements are found, the family must band together to support each other. All the previously suggested solutions should be implemented in this situation.

Problem 3: Leaving Home. This may be tougher on you than it is on your child! Regardless, the entry into the world is for most a rectangular period.

Solution: Don't cut the ties completely. Be available, even if just over the phone.

What to Expect from a Rectangle Child at Home

1. Ambivalence. He/She is unsure about everything.
2. Heavy influence of peers. This child often seeks to identify with others who appear stronger and more sure.
3. Hero worship. From rock stars to astronauts, this will continue through the rectangular period. It will pass.
4. "Momma's boy/girl" syndrome. Often a strong attachment to a parent develops out of the need for more security.
5. Low performance in school. During the rectangular period, do not expect good grades. There is too much going on in that confused mind to concentrate on school work.
6. Dominance over younger siblings. This is often the only way the rectangle child can assert control over something.
7. Copycat behavior of older siblings. With no firm direction of his/her own, this is highly likely.
8. Constant questions.

How to Raise a Rectangle Child

1. Reinforce the child's decisions whenever possible.
2. Celebrate accomplishments, large and small.
3. Be available to talk over problems/insecurities. This is *very* important with a rectangle child!
4. Establish a *stable* home environment. The outside world may be chaotic, but home is stable.

5. Provide siblings. Have other children in the family. A rectangular only child is a bigger problem.

6. Encourage outside activities: scouts, church, etc.

7. Be ready to be a chauffeur. Rectangle children should not be left to their own devices (or those of their peers).

8. *Most important of all*, give *unconditional love and support*! Give 150 percent to this child, during this rectangular period, and you will reap the rewards of a healthy, happy child in the future! The rectangular child who seemed like an "ugly duckling" to you may grow into a beautiful swan!

Chapter 12

The Rectangle at Work

Your rectangle co-worker, boss, subordinate is acting "weird." You don't quite know how to take him/her. One day he/she is spunky and full of life; the next he/she acts like a truck hit him/her. Rectangles are known by radical **mood shifts**. Their personalities can actually change from day to day. Everyone in the office learns to tread lightly when passing the office of the rectangle.

That's the bad news. The good is that your rectangle is only *going through a phase*. He/she will pass through it. It may be rough going during this period, but this chapter will help you to understand what's happening and why. It will help you learn how to deal with your rectangular colleague more effectively during this awkward phase.

The most common traits of people experiencing this transitional phase are: **searching, growing, inquisitive, exciting,** and **courageous.** The downside is that they are also **confused, changeable, inconsistent, gullible, ingenuine,** and **unpredictable.** Of course, as a co-worker, you must take the good with the bad!

The typical jobs in which one might locate a rectangle are:

new bosses	mid-life crisis people
entry-level employees/job applicants	performers (stage/music)
	entrepreneurs
fresh college/high school graduates	new retirees
	adolescents
newly promoted/demoted employees	housewives

If you are working with someone who displays the traits which identify a rectangle, this person may be a new boss, an entry-level employee, a fresh graduate, or a newly promoted or demoted person. Regardless of the situation, the rectangular characteristics of this person at work are difficult to deal with. Remember, this is a phase that your rectangle will pass through. There is light at the end of the tunnel!

HOW RECTANGLES DEAL WITH CONFLICT

Conflict is nothing new to the rectangle. He/she is feeling intense conflict within him/herself right now! Thus, when external conflict develops, it is doubly upsetting to the already convoluted rectangle.

The most typical rectangular response to conflict with co-workers is to **totally avoid it.** There is wisdom in this choice, because the rectangle is already confused and it is probably better not to get directly involved at this time.

However, the rectangle is a phase, and the person in it has been another shape before this. If conflict emerges, the most *natural behavior for the rectangle is to return to his/her former shape to deal with the conflict.* For example, if the rectangle was a triangle or squiggle in the past, he/she will be prone to confront the situation directly; if a circle, the tendency is to compromise. If the rectangle was a former box (this is the most likely), there will be an even stronger tendency to avoid the conflict!

However, since the rectangle is no longer a solid box, triangle, circle, or squiggle; his/her behavior during conflict is really *unpredictable.* As a co-worker, you will have to deal with the behavior you see at the moment. This is true in all interactions with rectangles. This is what makes them so very difficult to work with.

HOW TO WIN AN ARGUMENT WITH A RECTANGLE

1. Good Luck! What you argue about with a rectangle one day may change completely the next! He/she may change his/her mind or even totally forget the conversation! Whatever occurs, you will be smart to *put it in writing.* "CYA" is very important protection when working with rectangles.

2. Present a "Sure Front." Because rectangles are confused and unsure, they think others are also. They are more easily swayed by people who seem to have it all together.

3. Initiate the Confrontation! Remember, the rectangle is prone to avoid conflict. If you *must* get it worked out, you will have to insist upon the discussion.

4. Separate the Wheat from the Chaff. Often rectangles will engage in heated arguments over unimportant matters. This is because they are not sure what *is* important! Be willing to give in on these items. Save your strength for the things that really matter to you.

5. Keep It Focused. The rectangle will change the subject often, particularly if he/she senses that he/she is losing. You must bring it back to the problem at hand, and, be careful to define the problem precisely. The rectangle may be unclear as to the definition of the problem itself.

6. Hold the Discussion Outside the Office if at All Possible. The rectangle is easily distracted in the office itself.

7. Do Not Allow the Argument to Disintegrate into an Emotional Battle. The rectangle is already wearing his/her emotions on his/her sleeve. If it gets too heated, suggest a continuance at a later time.

8. Work for a Win/Win Solution. The rectangle has already lost face within his/her own mind. Find a way that the rectangle can at least preserve his/her pride.

9. Reinforce the Relationship Throughout. This will be important later when the rectangle comes out of this phase. Otherwise, the rectangle may blame you later for taking advantage of him/her when he/she was down.

10. Final Note: Don't Do Battle with a Rectangle Unless You Have To. This person is not him/herself. Whatever conclusion is reached, it may be completely overturned when the rectangle solidifies into another shape after passing through this stage.

THE RECTANGLE CO-WORKER

If you have to count on this person to get your job done, you have a problem! Characteristic of this shape are **inconsistency** and **unpredictability**. In an office situation where everyone has a certain job to do and each must depend upon the other, rectangles can cause havoc! They may know how to do the job and what is expected of them, but they want to change it! They often complain about the type or amount of work they must do. Even if they did the same work willingly in the past, they are suddenly dissatisfied with everything and everyone. They will cause problems without even realizing it. (Remember, the real problem is within the rectangle.)

Problem 1: "So, Who Is He/She Today?" Rectangles are mercurial in their ability to *change roles* from day to day (even within the same day).

Solution: Listen before you speak. Carefully discern which role the rectangle is presently playing. Then, adjust your communication to it. This puts an extra burden on you, but it works.

Problem 2: "We're Changing the Whole Procedure!" In a team leadership position, the rectangle can be deadly. They waffle on their decisions and may make dramatic changes in midstream.

Solution: Pose questions that make the rectangle stop and think. Force consideration of the implications of the rectangle's decision. If the rectangle is still primarily a left-brained shape, this analysis will be useful. Avoid sounding threatening, since this will force the rectangle to retreat.

Problem 3: "You Dropped the Ball." Because rectangles are so unsure of themselves, they often transfer those feelings to others. They may blame others for their own mistakes in judgment.

Solution: Certainly you must accept criticism if it is due; but, if it is not, be strong enough to rationally and calmly explain your perspective. If you must take the matter to a higher level of authority, do so.

Problem 4: "What Do You Think?" Rectangles may try to get others to make their decisions for them. They are vulnerable and unsure and are asking for help. The problem is that if you offer an idea and it doesn't work, the rectangle will blame you later.

Solution: Offer helpful suggestions whenever possible. But . . . . also remind the rectangle that he/she must take the ultimate responsibility for the decision.

Problem 5: "Can We Talk. . . . ?" Unfortunately, the rectangle is going through a difficult life stage. He/she needs to talk about it with someone. If there are few close personal friends or family members in his/her life, he/she may choose to unload on a friendly fellow worker.

Solution: Listen wisely. Do not allow the rectangle to dominate your time at work. Suggest that you meet to talk outside of the office. Be careful about giving any strong advice. Merely listen and act as a sounding board. If you give advice and it is wrong, you will get the blame later and the relationship will suffer. (*Note*: If you don't want to be put in this position at all, do not make yourself available. Many circles find themselves in the middle of rectangle problems and regret it later.)

Problem 6: "Gone again?" *Absenteeism* is a major problem with rectangles. They are often truly ill (sometimes accident prone). More often, they merely feel fatigued from the weight of their many problems.

Solution: Be ready to take up the slack. If at all possible, counsel the rectangle about his/her responsibility to others. The best bet is not to put the rectangle into a position where others must count on him/her during this time.

THE RECTANGLE BOSS

Every new boss experiences a rectangular period. This is merely a transition that the new bosses must pass through to become acquainted with their new jobs and comfortable in new leadership positions. It is the *learning curve* stage of development. The positive side of this is that you, as the subordinate during this period, have the opportunity to *influence the boss*.

This is a time he/she will be the most open and receptive to your ideas and suggestions.

In fact, some new bosses accomplish great and needed changes during their beginning phase because they are willing to listen to the employees. Some rectangles in this position are naively courageous and willing to challenge the "old ways" of doing it. They will take action that the former boss would never have taken. This opportunity to influence your boss may not come again.

Pluses

1. New in position; learning and growing
2. Inquisitive; willing to listen
3. Malleable; can be influenced
4. Courageous; will take a risk
5. Entertaining; likes to play act

Minuses

1. Naive to politics; gullible
2. Unpredictable changes
3. Mood swings are common
4. Too slow/fast to make decisions
5. Unsure of procedures; learning curve
6. Never know "where you stand" as employee

Note: The mood swings of the rectangle boss can be very difficult to deal with. They can be so severe that they are momentary changes in personality! For example, the new, unsure boss may metaphorically try on any one of the *other four shapes* on any given day. He/she may come to work as a flaming triangle, ready to do battle. He/she may bark orders then return to his/her office and feel bad about it. Later, the same boss may emerge as a soft circle and try to make up by being overly friendly to everyone. The rectangle can also display box or squiggle characteristics. Thus, if a rectangle is who you work for, you must decide on a daily basis, "Who is he/she today?"

How to Please Your Rectangle Boss

1. Do not **expect** anything; be ready for everything.
2. **Re-evaluate** your boss daily. Observe carefully for changes in mood and temperament. (Ask the secretary.)
3. Give time and space. **Don't push!**
4. Put proposals in **writing** and submit ahead of time for consideration.
5. Offer **suggestions** and **ideas**—boss is receptive.

6. Sense **vulnerability**; go in "for the kill" if you really want something done.

7. Stay informed at all times. Tap into the **political networks.** This boss may not make it.

8. Give **compliments;** the rectangle needs it. However, the boss will be suspicious of false compliments, so don't be effusive.

9. **Avoid arguments** if at all possible. This can have harmful repercussions after the rectangle period.

10. Expect **criticism.** Don't be defensive, the rectangle is more critical of him/herself.

11. Always have a new **joke** handy. Keeping the office atmosphere light will help everyone.

12. **Hang in there!** This is a transitional period; it will pass.

Final Note: Your rectangle boss may not be a *new* boss but may be someone who is experiencing one of the life stages which force people into rectangular periods (divorce, mid-life crisis, demotion, etc.) If this is true, the emotional component of the rectangle personality will be even more acute. You may want to pay close attention to Chapter Thirteen on the rectangle in stress.

THE RECTANGLE CUSTOMER

How to Identify a Rectangle Customer

1. You've seen him/her before—this is a frequent visitor. The rectangle can't decide, so will make several return trips. He/she may even ask some of the same questions about your product/service again.

2. This is the customer who looks out of place. Rectangles are uncomfortable with themselves and this is reflected wherever they are.

3. Shifting weight and nervous body language will give the rectangle away.

4. This customer will be timid at first, usually saying, "I'm just looking." Wait and try to help again later.

5. There is no set "costume" for the rectangle. He/she could be dressed like any one of the other four shapes. It's according to the mood of the day.

6. Tough to "peg." If you have a rectangle customer, this is the one you have trouble "pegging"—they change from visit to visit.

7. Doesn't listen. The rectangle will ask you a question then interrupt you in the middle of your answer to the question with another one. He/she doesn't seem to be following you.

8. This customer will jump from one product to the next. If you're

in a department store, you may end up selling things from several departments to this person.

9. Because the moods are erratic, this customer may appear to be friendly at first and suddenly turn cold and critical of your product/service.

10. Be ready to spend time. The rectangle usually won't decide to buy quickly. However, if the rectangle is in a triangular mood, he/she is capable of making an impulsive decision.

How to "Sell" a Rectangle Customer

1. **Probe.** Ask lots of questions to determine needs.

2. Be **concerned** when you detect confusion.

3. Be **clear** and **concise** in your communication. Don't add to the confusion. KISS it.

4. Demonstrate how your product/service will **simplify** life. The rectangle doesn't want anything more complicated.

5. Expect many **questions**, even repeated ones.

6. Be **patient;** it will take time.

7. Ask for the sale during a pause. If the rectangle doesn't respond the first time, repeat the attempt several times. However, don't overdo it, you'll scare this customer away easily.

8. Be aware of the rectangle's **gullibility.** Although you may want to stretch the truth a little about your product/service, don't overdo it.

9. **Verify** the rectangle's ability to pay. Rectangle's sometimes go on shopping sprees to solve their problems. They may purchase things they cannot afford.

10. **Secure** an appropriate **installation appointment,** and, advise the service staff to call first before going. The rectangle often forgets logistics, because there is so much confusion in other arenas of his/her life.

Final Note: Do not expect to develop a loyal customer out of a rectangle. These people are apt to buy things they don't really need, so, *returned merchandise* is also common. They will try different things and reject them when the mood changes.

Chapter 13

___ The Rectangle Under Stress

The rectangular shape is stress personified! It is the person who is experiencing a major life change. Although this period of his/her life brings excitement and variety, it also brings the stress of adaptation to new circumstances and situations. This will be the most important chapter in the section for rectangles and for those who live with them.

How to Identify a Rectangle Under Stress

As with the other four shapes, when stress emerges, the *negative traits* of the shape become the most visible. In the case of the rectangle, the following behaviors intensify:

1. **Confusion.** This is the most characteristic of the rectangular shape. Whereas in the past this person was much more confident and sure of him/herself, now he/she seems incapable of making the smallest decision. The rectangle will "waffle" from day to day. Today, he/she is sure that this is the thing to do. Tomorrow, he/she changes his/her mind. The rectangle under stress will be **forgetful, unsure,** and **distracted.** Although to some degree, this is characteristic of the shape itself, these traits will *intensify under stress.*

2. **Low Self-Esteem.** This is really the *bottom-line!* This is the reason for all of the other problems. It is actually the source of the rectangle shape. There is usually a *cause* for the loss of normal self-esteem and self-confidence. If the rectangle can deduce the cause, then he/she can take concrete action to rebuild his/her self-esteem. However, until the rectangle is clear about why he/she is rejecting the "old" ways of behaving, this stage will continue. The longer it continues, the more stress will develop.

2. **Mood Swings.** Under stress, this expands to violent displays of temper and ecstatic periods of joy. These emotions can emerge within seconds

of one another. They can be triggered by small things, sometimes seeming to have no basis in reality. Since the rectangle is already moody, under stress he/she demonstrates mood swings in the extreme. Of course, this is very difficult to deal with on the part of the rectangle's friends and work associates. (Dealing with these periods will be discussed later in this chapter.)

3. Changeable/Inconsistent/Unpredictable. Each of these characteristics becomes more evident when the rectangle is at the height of his/her stress.

a. Changeable: The rectangle can take on the characteristics of any of the other four shapes at any time.

b. Inconsistent: The rectangle will tell you that he/she didn't say this or agree to that yesterday. You know this may not be the truth, but you must understand that the rectangle just doesn't remember it. You cannot depend on a rectangle during this time.

c. Unpredictable: You cannot predict the behavior of a rectangle. The mood swings are instrumental in this. Because the rectangle is in such a severe state of change, he/she can become a different person everyday. It would be foolish to attempt to predict his/her behavior, since the rectangle him/herself doesn't know what to expect on a daily basis.

4. Gullible. During this searching, growing, changing period, the rectangle is also the most **suggestible**. This is because he/she is **open to new learning**. This is a wonderful time for this person to be in school where he/she can learn new concepts in a structured way.

However, there are those people who would take advantage of the rectangle during this period. Those who would **manipulate** the gullible rectangle to their own advantage. A stressful rectangle will believe anything during this period and may make some changes in his/her life that are ultimately harmful. Getting involved with the "wrong people" or the wrong group must be guarded against.

5. Ingenuine. This characteristic is merely an outgrowth of the rectangle's need to change for the better. It manifests itself through **role-playing** and **play-acting**. The rectangle may play the "tough guy" role one day and the "shrinking violet" the next. Some of this role-playing is actually *purposeful* as the rectangle searches for *redefinition of self*.

Most of it is merely play-acting just to get the feel of how it would be to be a person like that. Some rectangles actually take on the characteristics of other people—a friend, parent, or even a movie star. This is not to be taken seriously unless the rectangle actually begins to believe that he/she *is* the other person. It is rare that the rectangle will lock into becoming someone else because of the inconsistency of his/her daily behavior.

Rectangles have been known to seek out new people and places where they are not known. They do this to find a "testing ground" for their new role. For example, I once knew a heavily stressed rectangle who went to a new bar every night after work and told the people he met there that he was a different person. One night, he would be a truck driver, the next a professor, the next a pilot, and so on. This was a "safe" way for him to role-play. *Please note*: This does *not* mean that the rectangle is schizophrenic. Most rectangles are merely seeking outlets in which they can safely try on new "selves" and see how they fit. They become *restless* in their need to change.

So, what about the old self, the person the rectangle was before he/she entered this transitional period? That too will occasionally emerge, but it will be instantly rejected because that is the person with whom the rectangle is displeased. It's why this stage of life occurs! It's also one reason why rectangles often seek out new friends and acquaintances, because the old ones keep trying to communicate with the rectangle's "former self," the one he/she wants to discard.

Sources of Stress for Rectangles

The world! Since the primary source of stress for the rectangle is *within him/herself*, almost every interaction with others becomes stressful for him/her. However, there are some predictable *life circumstances* that cause the most normal people to enter or intensify a rectangular state. For ease of understanding, I have divided them into work-related and personal life-related categories.

Work-Related Sources

1. **Major Job Change.** This can be put into several subcategories as follows:

   a. Change in nature of job. This requires new learning and adaptation. If the rectangle is middle-aged or beyond, and the change is great, this will cause great stress. Likewise, if the job is too difficult, or one for which the employee has no training or experience.

   b. Change in company/location. Many corporations routinely move their employees (management) from one city to the next. They are often unaware of the stressful burden this places on both the employee and his/her family. The result is that *the only stability is the company!*

2. **Change in Job Status.**

   a. Promotion. Although people seek promotions and receive them with honor, they are also stressful periods. Most prominent is the promotion that brings one to the first position of authority—the "new boss." In this situation, not only must the rectangle adapt to a new job, but also he/she must establish him/herself in a leadership position.

b. Demotion. Although easier if it is self-inflicted (done by choice), demotion is rarely stressless. The accepted norm in this society is "upward mobility." Thus, when someone is demoted, the assumption of others is that something is wrong with that person. The "demotee" will then enter a rectangular period to stop and re-evaluate him/herself.

Personal-Life Sources

Divorce	Strained marital relationship
Death of loved one	First baby
Major illness	Child leaving home
Marriage	Parent living in household
Parenting problem	Serious financial problems

It should be noted that any one on the personal-life sources of stress can cause problems, but if more than one is happening at the same time, the stress can be severe.

Stressful People for Rectangles

1. **Triangles.** They are the number one source of people-stress for rectangles. The reason is simple—the triangle is very sure of him/herself, this sense of confidence being the one quality the rectangle lacks and wants most. Please note: The rectangle has greatest difficulty dealing with triangles *when he/she has been a triangle in the past.* Then the envy for his/her lost self-confidence is most acute.

2. **Squiggles.** These people intensify the *confusion* in the rectangle. Because the right-brained squiggle naturally jumps from one thing to another, the rectangle (who is left-brain dominant), becomes more confused when communicating with this person.

3. **Boxes.** Particularly if the rectangle is truly a box in transition to a triangle, box people will be stressful to him/her during this period. This is the shape he/she hopes to reject. Thus, the old saying . . . . "We are most critical of our own faults manifested in others."

4. **Old Friends.** This is an important category of stress for rectangles because during this period of change, old friends remind them of the "past self" they are attempting to reject. This puts pressure on old friendships and sometimes the damage becomes irreversible.

Note: The most positive shape for the rectangle under stress is the **circle.** This understanding and compassionate person is willing to help and listen. It is actually to the rectangle's benefit to *seek out circles* during this transitional period. One of the most common causes of divorce during the rectangular period is the replacement of a triangular spouse with a circular one! The rectangle says, "Now I have someone who cares about *me!*" Whether or not this is true, it is the rectangle's perception and it reflects the intense need of the rectangle to be appreciated for him/herself.

How the Rectangle Deals with Stress

1. **The Most Common Behavior Is the Rectangle's Almost Daily Personality Changes.** The simplest way to describe this is that the rectangle can "become" any one of the other four shapes at any time. This is the demonstration of the rectangle's *restless search* to better him/herself.

The rectangle is actually "role-playing" each of the other shapes. If the "audience" consistently applauds for one shape over the other, this may be the final "role" the rectangle will play.

2. **Illness/Injury.** This is likely during this period. Not a pleasant thought, but rectangles often tend to be accident-prone. In their new-found role, they may be courageous enough to try new activities never tried before. If they do not sufficiently prepare, they can easily hurt themselves.

3. **Manic-Depressive Mood Changes.** This is the toughest one to deal with for those who must live with the rectangle during his/her transition. Unless friends and associates are apprised of the rectangle's state of mind, these severe mood changes can do long-term damage to their relationships. When the rectangle finally passes through his/her painful transition and rebuilds his/her self-esteem, he/she may look around and be surprised to find very few friends left!

4. **Suicidal.** Although this is *very rare*, the rectangle may become suicidal if his/her self-esteem plummets to it's lowest ebb. If you have any suspicion that this is a possibility, then you must help the rectangle to seek *professional help* immediately!

How to Help Your Rectangle to Reduce Stress

1. Seek **psychological professional help** if you feel that your rectangle is about to go off the deep end.

2. Seek **medical help** at the first sign of any serious physical illness or accident.

3. Watch your rectangle closely if there is any precipitating **traumatic event** that occurs during this time.

4. Be a **constant support** to your rectangle in every way possible. However, encourage him/her to rebuild his/her own self-respect and esteem. Ultimately he/she must do it for him/herself; no one else can do it for him/her.

5. If you sense that the need for change is job-related, **encourage a job change.** Bring home literature about other types of work.

6. If possible, shift the **financial burden** to your own shoulders during this period. This may be a mitigating factor in the rectangle's need for a change.

7. Introduce your rectangle to **new friends** in other fields of interest. This will assist him/her in the search process for a different line of work, and, it will fill the rectangle's need to "role play" new selves with a new audience.

8. Encourage new and different **outside activities** into the rectangle's life. This serves as a pleasant distraction to his/her problems and fulfills the need to explore and to experience new things.

9. Provide some **comic relief** if at all possible. Attend only comedy movies and plays. Surround your rectangle with "upbeat" people. Keeping it light will take the edge off to some degree.

10. **Inform friends and family members** (maybe even work associates) about what is taking place. These people must interact with your rectangle also, and they need to know that the problem is not with them—it is within the rectangle. (This is particularly important if children are involved. They will tend to blame themselves and develop undeserved guilt.)

Final Note: Be sure to reinforce your own *personal support system* of friends and associates during this trying time. You will need support yourself! Remember, even if it gets bad, this is a *transitional period*. It will pass! Your support now is more needed than ever. Give it unquestioningly and without reservation. If you do, you will have a healthy, positive relationship with your rectangle when the entire experience is over.

Rectangles Feel Most Comfortable When . . . .

1. They are **learning** something new.
2. They sense the **excitement of change** within themselves.
3. They can **fantasize** positive outcomes to their problems.
4. They have the **freedom to explore** themselves through alternative careers and relationships.
5. They are **financially secure** enough to ride out the changes.
6. There is a **healthy balance** in their lives giving them the time for both **stimulation** and **reflection.**
7. They are **physically** and **psychologically healthy.**
8. They have a strong and loving **support system** of friends, family, and associates around them.
9. They feel **safe** in a world that will allow them to change.
10. They have an overall **positive attitude** toward the future.

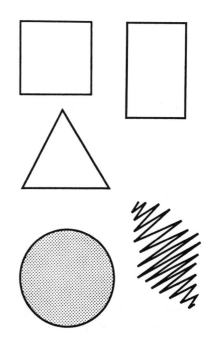

Section Four

THE GREGARIOUS CIRCLE

Chapter 14

Identifying the Circle . . . . The Ole Smoothie

Belief: "Do unto others as you would have others do unto you."

Translation: If everyone would just *love* one another, this world would be a better place in which to live.

I call you circles the **lovers** among us! People are your number one concern, and you will try to keep **harmony** at all costs—usually your own. Mythologically, the circle is symbolic of harmony and, in my observation, this tends to be true of you popular circles. You will notice that much of this section will revolve around *people*: This is due to the circle's primary focus on others. You will learn why (even after your best efforts) there are certain individuals you simply cannot win over. It is important for you to note the aspects of your shape that directly intrude upon your ability to be effective in a leadership position. You may want to consider these, for they are correctable with some effort on your part.

OVERVIEW

The circle person is the most **friendly** of the five shapes. This is because circles are genuinely interested in others. They are the best **communicators** because they are the best listeners. They "read" people well, and they establish **empathy** quickly with them. A circle will actually "feel" your pain with you; and, when he/she does, the circle will **nurture** you back to health, if at all possible. People with problems naturally gravitate to circles. Many of the helping professions are full of circles for this reason. (See list, Chapter Sixteen.)

Circles have their greatest difficulty in life when they must deal with human *conflict*. Circles want everyone to get along and to like one another. When the circle has a conflict with someone, it is the circle who is most likely to give in first. A common circular trait is **accommodating** others. Although this pleases others and makes the circle **popular,** it can often lead to the circle's loss of self-respect. This must be guarded against.

If the issue is one of morale or treating people right, the circle becomes impassioned in his/her plea. Circles can be very **persuasive** when they want to. Circles with a strong triangular leaning have the ability to become *charismatic leaders*. However, the pure circle lacks the left-brained, organizational skills of his/her linear brothers. Rather than the leader, this shape is more often found as the **stabilizer** of the group. The circle is more concerned with harmony than with destiny.

Circles are altogether pleasant to be around and try their best to please others. They must be careful not to neglect themselves in the process, as they tend to become **reflective** and **self-denigrating** when things go wrong.

QUICK INDICATORS OF CIRCLE PEOPLE

Language

Common Words: lovely, nice, feel, gut-level, complimentary, comfortable, helpful, cooperate, team.

Common Sayings: "We're one big happy family around here!" "No problem." "I'm snowed under, but I'll find a way to help you out." "Let's sit down and talk it over." "People are our most important Product!"

Appearance

Men: Casual. The emphasis is on *comfort*. The circle man shuns the three-piece-suit look and prefers the sports jacket (brown corduroy with leather elbow patches is perfect), open-neck shirt and no tie. Circles like "earth colors" of brown, tan and green; they also like some blues and burgundies. He is unconcerned with the fads, labels, etc. He likes time-worn clothing that feels good, like an old friend. Unconcerned with making an impression. (Can do it if he needs to "fit in," however.)

The circle carries an handkerchief in case he meets some "damsel in distress." He shuns flashy jewelry, but would never forget to wear his wedding ring. Commitments to people are important. At home, he is found in turtleneck sweaters and comfortable slacks or jeans. There is often an enviable youthful fleshy face with an *overweight* tendency. There is a noticeable lack of facial worry lines.

Some circles try to look older by sporting a full beard. I have a friend who is a university professor and recently removed his full beard of 15 years. His wife thought she was living with a stranger! He dropped 10 years immediately. She was upset because she thought he looked younger than she! She laughingly told friends there was no "truth in packaging."

Women: Again, the casual theme is dominant. Both circle men and women hate to dress up. Women are not your "Dress for Success" variety. They wear more loose-fitting, feminine fabrics that feel good to the skin: sweaters, jersey, angora, light wool, etc. Circle women are often found in full, flowing skirts and blouses with bows and fluffs. A layered look is common. Colors are primarily pastels and earth tones. Hair is usually curly and short or quite long. Circle women (as with most women) tend to be more faddish than the men. Painted fingernails are common and perfume scents are strong and sweet-smelling.

Like her male counterpart, the circle woman ages well. She is also less concerned with appearance in later years than her linear sisters; the "natural" look is preferred. However, she will acquire early facial lines around the eyes and mouth, a result of excessive *smiling* throughout life. She wouldn't dream of removing those lines and feels that she earned them. On stressful days at the office, the circle woman's hairstyle may fall a bit and she may show signs of wear, but her smile will dominate those hardened lines around the eyes that hint of martyrdom.

Office

When you visit a circle, you will think you just walked into someone's home. The circle's office is decorated with lots of live plants. It is done in soft colors or earth tones. Since circles prefer overstuffed furniture to heavy wooden structures, there is usually a couch or loveseat with lots of pillows. Comfort for the visitor is the primary concern.

The work space is a bit disorganized with papers strewn about somewhat haphazardly. The desk area is filled with photos of people goofing off together (the last company picnic or Christmas party). Of course the last four family reunions are there also. There may be cut flowers or cards on the desk (a recent gift from an thankful co-worker who had a problem that the circle helped to solve). Of course, there is an extra jacket or raincoat hanging behind the door—as much for others who might need it as for the circle him/herself. This is a person with the needs of others in mind at all times.

Personal Habits

1. Face-to-Face Communication. The circle uses all five senses with people and needs to work with them directly to activate this sensory reading. Because the circle concentrates intensely, one person at a time is preferred.

2. **Easy-going.** Circles tend to be jolly, fun-loving people. They are the first to "belly up to the bar" and the last to leave it. As long as everyone is having fun, the circle loves it.

3. **Joiner.** It is the circles who join the clubs and organizations and derive a great deal of pleasure from doing so. Although they rarely become the "president," they are always in charge of the social events.

4. **Recreation Preferences Are Small Group Gatherings with a Few Close Friends and Associates.** (Associates *are* friends). Golf, bicycling, cards and games are preferred over more competitive, fast-action sports.

5. **Old-fashioned.** Circles are sentimental sorts. They save things like scrapbooks, letters, pressed corsages, family heirlooms, and old clothes. The circle probably has his/her first dollar bill.

6. **Complimentary.** If you want a real "shot in the arm," go see a circle. Circles are believers in people and they tend to be highly complimentary of others.

7. **Reading Habits.** The circle subscribes to *People, Life, Readers' Digest,* and *National Geographic.* He/she often reads the *National Inquirer* secretly in the grocery line and watches lots of TV (and can easily become hooked on soap operas).

8. **Hobbies.** Circles like crafts, gardening and fixing things. I have known many circles who wrote poetry and some short stories. They tend to lack the discipline to write a full book.

9. **Sloppy.** In terms of personal habits, you often have to follow along behind a circle and pick up the mess. It's not that he/she intends to be sloppy. Neatness is just not a high priority.

10. **Good Cook.** A natural outgrowth of the need to please people, circles combine food and socializing. Not thinking of themselves as gourmets, just good home cookin'. (This may also contribute to their tendency for being overweight.)

Body Language

1. **Smiling . . . .** at everyone, indiscriminately at 8 A.M.!

2. **Head Nodding and Bobbing to Show Support and Acceptance of Others.** When accompanied with smiling, the circle can appear overly subordinate or even (in women) flirtatious.

3. **Body Mirroring.** The circle will concentrate on you intensely and unconsciously "mirror" your body posture and movements. Many counselors are taught this technique as part of their training.

4. **Full Eye Contact to the Point of Staring.** Since the upper end of "average" eye contact between people is 80 percent, the circle tends to exceed this and sometimes makes others uncomfortable.

5. **High Touch.** Oh yes . . . . this is the "touchy-feely" person. Circles are often seen with their arms around co-workers.

6. **Cupped Handshake.** Circles feel that shaking hands is too *formal* a greeting, but when forced to do it, they will embellish the handshake by cupping the other person's hand in both of theirs. They may also grab the upper arm muscle during the handshake to demonstrate the affection they are feeling.

7. **Bouncy Stride.** Circles show their positive attitude in their posture and walk. They will also tend to pace their stride to that of the person walking with them.

8. **Mellow Voice.** The circle's voice is usually low-pitched and melodic. It is easily listened to. The rate of speech is slow and smooth. The voice impression is comforting and relaxed.

9. **Endomorphic Body Shape.** Anthropologically-speaking, this means the person tends to be big-boned with wide hips and long torso. The limbs are usually shorter than average. Medium height to short and stocky is standard.

10. **Attractive.** Many others perceive circles to be highly physically attractive people. I am persuaded that this impression is as much because of the circle personality as the actual physical appearance of the circle.

SUMMARY

Well-liked by everyone, the circle "rolls" through life spreading good will all around him/her. This person is the expert in "smoothing ruffled feathers" and persuading others to work together more harmoniously. The circle is nurturing, caring, team-oriented, empathic, stabilizing, persuasive, reflective, and *everyone's favorite person.*

Although the circle shares these qualities freely with others, he/she is not always as kind to him/herself! When something goes wrong, the circle tends to *blame self first.* A circle has a tendency to denigrate him/herself to the point of heavy **melancholy** and even severe depression. This trait is the one that is most damaging to the circle and one against which the circle must guard.

The circle *blends the personal with the professional* and tends to make co-workers into personal friends. Although this is pleasant, it can erode the circle's job performance. It is particularly difficult for circles to deal with **conflict,** either at work, or at home. Their shape is symbolic of world **harmony** and **peace.** In later years, the true circle can develop an incredible **wisdom** about life and people. There is a deeper significance to the circle as the symbol of integration and psychic (even mystical) wholism of body and soul. *Circles have a great deal to offer to this world.*

Overall, the life of the circle is an enviable series of applause from all who know him/her. From homemade cinnamon rolls to flowers on your birthday, you can't go wrong with a relationship with a circle. Your discussions will have depth and, when you need it, you will be tenderly nurtured and cared for. Enjoy your circles, they make the world go 'round!

Chapter 15

The Circle at Home

Lucky you! If there is a strong circle in your home environment, you can ask for little more. This is the person who truly cares about others; whose primary purpose in life is to help, nurture, and serve. *The home is the province of the circle!* Classic circles could be called homebodies.

It should be noted that even if the person you live with does not demonstrate circular characteristics at work, he/she may be a circle at home. Our society teaches the value of "Home, Sweet Home." In this busy world, this is the one place that we can relax, let our hair down, and allow the milk of human kindness to flow from us. Thus, even some of the most dictatorial triangles at work can become pussycats at home. This is the one place they can let their guard down, show tenderness, even be vulnerable and admit mistakes.

I point this out because many times I have heard wives or husbands describe their spouse as a "total circle," and, yet, the co-workers of this person would completely disagree. To them, he/she was a total triangle or box! This is particularly true in the case of a circle at home who may be a different shape entirely at work. (It is certainly possible that *a person may be one shape at work, and a different shape at home.*)

THE CIRCLE SPOUSE

The circle spouse is caring, sensitive, and puts others first. When there is conflict at home, this spouse will accommodate the needs of others. This person is sometimes *generous to a fault* and will truly give you the shirt off his/her back.

Circles need people in their lives, so, they prefer large families. If this is not possible, they will turn friends into family. When you visit the home of a circle, there are always people there; friends, neighbors, co-workers, it doesn't matter. The circle will sit them all down at the kitchen table and treat them like royalty. The circle is the best host of all five shapes. You will always feel comfortable in a circle's home.

How to Create an Ideal Circle Home

1. **Comfort First!** The home decor should reflect the circular shape—curved lines. Furniture should be upholstered (overstuffed chairs and "pit" groups) reflecting a smooth, rounded feeling. No flashy metals and cold glass for the warm circle. Circles like the "great room" for entertaining.

2. **Earth Colors Are Preferred.** The warm tones of brown, orange, red, mauve, and green are the ones circles feel best in.

3. **Many Circles Like Antiques.** This is an outgrowth of their love of history and things that their ancestors have touched. Since circles are the most oriented to the past, their homes are often filled with heirlooms.

4. **Family Photos and Numerous Photos of Friends and Associates "at Play" Will Decorate the Home.** Circles are the ones who create the photo gallery throughout the hallway that leads to the bedrooms. Circles often have family portraits done to hang over the fireplace. (Triangles have a portrait of themselves there!) In fact, circles rarely write a letter without enclosing the latest photos of the family.

5. **Trinkets and Ceramic Figures Often Adorn Circle Homes.** Circles are the ones who buy the Hummel figures. They often have doll collections as well.

6. **Books and Magazines Adorn the Circle Home.** Circles are often avid readers of novels on romance, history, and mysteries.

7. **There Must a Secretary in the Corner of the Room for the Plethora of Correspondence the Circle Participates in.** Circles prefer personalized stationary embossed in script. They are constantly writing letters to their multitude of friends.

8. **Don't Expect Your Circle Spouse to Be Neat and Tidy.** People are more important than things, so circles tend to be a bit **sloppy** with pillows and afghans thrown around. Remember, circles are basically *lazy*.

9. **Few Established Routines.** The circle doesn't set routines because he/she must be open to the changing needs of others. You can call a circle at a moment's notice and he/she will be there.

10. **No Tight Budget for the Circle.** Circles must have a large "slush fund" for unexpected needs: anniversaries, birthdays, housewarmings, new babies, etc. Circles are generous **gift givers**. Their lack of attention to detail means that the checkbook rarely balances. They really don't care. Circles aren't into being rich. They just want to have enough to attract others to them.

11. **Circles Who Drove the Station Wagons in the '60s, Drive the Vans Today.** They must have a **large automobile** so that they are capable of transporting lots of people.

12. **There Must Be a Large Supply of a Variety of Foods in the House at All Times.** You never know what the guests will like. Circles often keep lots of snack foods on hand. They serve large portions of food because they live in fear of not having enough food to go around. Circles prefer home-cooked meals to gourmet restaurants.

Recreation for the Circle

1. **Large Family Parties Are the Norm, with Friends Included Also.** (Friends are like family to circles.) The circle prefers parties in the home. Small to medium sized groups of five to fifty will do. The more the merrier.

2. **Camping Is a Favorite of Circles.** They enjoy sitting casually around the campfire telling stories and singing songs. Of course, they enjoy meeting new people of all sorts.

3. **Circles Like to Combine Food with Socialization.** They prefer a long, drawn out meal in which the guests can be unhurried. Favorites for circles are outdoor barbecues, mulled wine and cheese by the fire, and fondue, of course.

4. **Circles Like Theme Parties.** Halloween is an all-time favorite. They love to play charades and are the new enthusiasts of the recently popular "murder parties."

5. **Circles Prefer Non-competitive Sports, of Course.** They will play team sports as long as the group is doing it for fun and winning isn't everything.

6. **The Circle Is a Joiner.** So he/she often belongs to recreational groups such as ski clubs, bridge clubs, travel clubs, even spas. Recreation is no fun for circles unless they can do it with others.

7. **Hobbies Are Low on the List, But the Circle Often Makes Gifts for Others (ceramics, for example), and Is Often a Collector.** I know a circle with a large "pig" collection (circles tend to be overweight). They also like *pets* of all types.

8. **Circles Are the Most Religious of the Five Shapes.** If they belong to an organized church, they usually become heavily involved in church activities. They tithe also.

9. **Circles Are Ardent Volunteers for Everything.** If any group or civic association needs help, the circle is the first one to raise his/her hand. Circles prefer to give their time rather than money. In this way, they have the opportunity to be seen by others and appreciated for their efforts.

10. **A Heavy TV Watcher, the National Networks Are Constantly Appealing to the Programming Tastes of Circles.** Circles prefer situation comedies

and historical movies. They are the biggest fans of "Highway to Heaven."

11. *Circles Subscribe to Lots of Magazines and Book Clubs.* They prefer *People* and *Reader's Digest,* and have been loyal members of *National Geographic* for years.

12. *When It Comes to Taking a Vacation, the Circle Chooses Group Events with His/Her Club, or Tours of Any Sort.* Cruises are OK too. Something like the "Bahama-rama" appeals to circles.

13. *Circles Are Heavy Convention Attendees.* They go not to learn more about their profession, but to party all night with colleagues and new associates. More subdued circles can get really wild at the out-of-state national convention.

14. *Finally. . . . of All the Five Shapes, the Circle Is Most Capable of Relaxing and Doing Nothing at All.* This drives a triangle or a box crazy, but the circle is perfectly content lying on the beach all day or just lazily puttering around the house all weekend with no particular plans.

If the truth were known, *the world has become much too busy and hectic for the circle.* The circle remembers the days when the town fathers sat in the barbershop to "chew the fat" all afternoon and the ladies enjoyed a leisurely 10 A.M. coffee together. Circles are the purveyors of the importance of the family unit and eschew this fast-moving society that rejects the more traditional values and habits of the past.

What to Expect from Your Circle Spouse

Pluses

1. Lots of love.
2. Genuine concern. Circles will put you first!
3. Active listening. As long as you want to talk, the circle will listen.
4. Loyalty. (Except for that occasional convention fling.)
5. Commitment. This is a very important word to circles. As members of a group, circles are committed to the people in the group, *not* to the club, organization, or company itself.
6. Nurturing. The circle is the "earth mother" and loves to be *needed* by others. He/she will nurture, nurse, caretake all forms of wounded creatures.
7. Compromise. Whenever there is conflict, the circle will seek a win/win solution. He/she will give in to the demands of others—sometimes too readily.
8. Generosity . . . . both with time and material things. Watch out, your circle spouse may give away everything you own if others need it!

9. Trust. Circles can be trusting to a fault. This is how more powerful others take advantage of them.

Minuses

1. Guilt. Circles suffer from this emotion and sometimes transfer it to others.

2. Self-denigration. When something goes wrong, the circle blames him/herself first.

3. Wishy-washy parenting. This often causes a problem for a child who needs more definite direction and a firm hand.

4. Illogical decisions. Circles make decisions based on their emotions and the feelings of others.

5. Motormouth. Circles love to talk about it. Many spouses say, "He/she never shuts up!"

6. Gossipy. Watch what you tell a circle. The circle must find things to talk about and the subject may be you!

7. Manipulative. When circles want their way, they are skilled at playing on the emotions of others to get it.

8. Over-emotional. Circular women can cry at the drop of a hat. Men often sulk.

9. Gullible. The negative side of the circle's need to trust people is that he/she can be easily persuaded to believe a lie.

How to "Accentuate the Positive" in Your Circle Spouse

1. **Assume the Responsibility for Major Decisions in the Home;** particularly when family members disagree. This is a burden that the circle will gladly relinquish, because he/she does not want to feel guilty about not pleasing everyone.

2. **Reveal Yourself.** Circles need to "know" people. They do not feel comfortable with people who are tight-lipped and mysterious. You must *be present* for a circle spouse.

3. **Be Honest.** Circles want and need to trust others. They will trust easily, but if their trust is broken, they can be vicious in seeking revenge.

4. **Ask Forgiveness.** If you do make a mistake, it is much better to admit it and ask forgiveness of your circle. Circles love to forgive, but hate to be lied to.

5. **Trust Your Circle's Judgment, Particularly About People.** Circles "read" people well and are usually very accurate in their assessment of others. This applies to problems with your children and friends.

6. **Take Responsibility for the Financial Decisions.** The circle is not

skilled here and will be pleased to be released from this burden. Keep track of small expenditures.

7. Ignore Some of the Circle's Moods. When you know your circle is being irrational about it, don't add fuel to the fire. Let him/her sulk awhile, but don't reinforce it.

8. Let Your Circle Know That It Is Not His/Her Fault! Circles will blame themselves first, and they often lack objectivity when there is a problem. You must contribute the objective point of view; be a rational *sounding board*.

9. Openly Discuss Family Problems. Don't push them under the rug. Get it out in the open and discuss it together.

10. Do Not Insist Upon an Immaculate House. Learn to live with yesterday's dishes, or wash them yourself!

11. Discourage the "Bleeding Heart" Tendency in Your Circle. Circles can overdo their involvement in the problems of others and they sometimes become over-involved in social issues.

12. Buffer Your Children Against Trying to Have Their Way Through Babytalk and Manipulation. Children are quick to learn what works with parents. These techniques will often work with circles and cause problems for the child years later.

13. Get Your Circle Out of the House! Circles tend to be homebodies and can become hermits. Convince your spouse to try new things and get out of the old rut. Be sure that your circle gets enough exercise. They tend not to.

14. Insist on Some Private Time for Yourself. If permitted to do so, the circle will monopolize you and everyone else.

15. Learn to Relax and Enjoy the "Type B" Circle Personality. Don't push and develop great expectations for your circle. Circles tend not to be ambitious, and they become nervous when they are around driven, anxious personalities. If you are a "Type A," don't expect your spouse to be like you.

16. Always Let Your Circle Spouse Know That He/She Is Loved and Needed for Him/Herself! This is the most important thing that you must do to maintain your relationship.

HOW TO FIND A CIRCLE MATE

Places to Find Circles

1. In the neighbor's front room on a regular basis.
2. At surprise parties; the circle is the host.
3. Local bars.

4. On vacation with relatives and/or friends.
5. In the barbershop or beauty parlor.
6. At the nursing home or hospital visiting the less fortunate.
7. On the boy/girl scout or big brother/sister board of directors.
8. At the local summer church/school camp as a counselor.
9. On the floor of the bar at a convention.
10. Carrying a sign in the protest march to save the whales, gays, homeless, you-name-it.
11. At home in front of the TV.

What to Say to a Circle

1. "I'm really close to my family, how about you?"
2. "What was it like—growing up in a small town?"
3. "What was the real problem in your first marriage?" (Circles get personal quickly.)
4. "Do you think it's OK for political candidates to cry?"
5. "Did you see the ABC special on abused children/battered wives? Isn't that terrible?"
6. "What did your horoscope say today? Were you supposed to meet an attractive stranger?"
7. "What did you think of the remake of *Gone with the Wind?*"
8. "How do you think we could improve relations with the Soviets?"
9. "Isn't apartheid deplorable?"
10. "Tell me all about your friends."

What to Do on the First Date

1. Talk, talk, talk.
2. Reveal a few of your deepest secrets/fears.
3. Bring your family album.
4. Go to a movie about social injustice. Allow plenty of time to talk about it afterwards.
5. Tell a sad story from your childhood. Be sure to muster a tear or two as you tell it.
6. Describe five parties that you attended within the last week.
7. Ask questions about the circle's life and listen very intently to whatever is said.

8. Stop for ice cream on the way home from the date.

9. Give him/her a lingering embrace at the door, then quickly leave.

How to Approach the "Sexual Question" with a Circle

1. First, it must be thoroughly *discussed* with a circle.

2. Be prepared to strip yourself of all guile and dirty deeds to be "worthy" of sexual acceptance by a circle.

3. Read all about "modern relationships" and use these words constantly.

4. Pledge undying "care" (love is not necessary in the beginning).

5. Choose the appropriate night and make it "romance plus!" You must court a circle in the old-fashioned sense.

6. Send flowers daily for a week before the marriage proposal.

7. Plan the wedding at least six months in advance. No whirlwind courtships for circles, they want to savor the entire emotional experience.

8. Meet the parents and family early; and make a good impression. These people do influence your circle.

9. Invite the entire city to your wedding. Be prepared to spare no expense. This will hold true for every important life event during your marriage to a circle.

Final Note: Enjoy your loving circle. This is the best shape for a partner. You will always come first in his/her life. As the poets say, "That's what love is about!"

THE CIRCLE CHILD

There is no more loving and openly affectionate child than a circle. He/she is a joy to every parent. However, there are some problems which may arise with this type of child, and caution is advised in handling them without destroying this most sensitive young person.

Problem 1: Need to Please Others. At first glance, this appears to be a positive quality, and it is. However, the circle can take it to the extreme. The child can become very upset when he/she is displeasing to others. Another form of this problem is the circular child's vulnerability to *peer pressure* later in young adulthood.

Solution: Teach the child that he/she is not going to please all the people all the time. This is hard learning for a circle, but very necessary. The child must learn to be *true to him/herself* and strong enough to reject the desires of others that may be harmful. As a parent, you must carefully monitor the child's friends to be sure they do not lead the child into drugs, etc. Some circular teen-age girls become pregnant in order to please! The circle child must learn to take an *unpopular stand* when self-protection requires it. If not learned early, the problem can manifest itself years later as people continue to step on the circle as an adult.

Problem 2: Hypersensitivity. Circles cry alot. They wear their feelings on their sleeves. As small children, their toys are taken from them. As teens, it seems that the world is out to get them and nobody likes them.

Solution: Do not allow this overly sensitive child to dissuade you from the proper discipline he/she must receive. However, do realize that this child will tend to be tougher on him/herself than you will be. Take this into account and discourage emotional flogging. Discuss problems in a logical, analytic manner; provoke the child's use of the left-brain when dealing with emotional issues.

Problem 3: Loneliness. Circles need people around them. If your circle child is an only child or alone a great deal of the time, this can be difficult for him/her. Many circle children develop imaginary playmates and/or treat stuffed animals as people in order to have companionship.

Solution: Have more than one child or, at least, provide as many play-mates as possible. You also will have to make an extra effort to make yourself available; this is particularly important if you are a single parent. It may be a good idea to live close to other family members during a single period. Divorce is extremely hard for a circular child who needs the love of both parents.

Problem 4: Demands Attention. Again, this reflects the circle child's need for people. This is most difficult in the preschool years. A circle baby may cry a lot; the older child may display abnormal behavior just to get attention.

Solution: Again, the more people who live with the circular child, the more the need for attention is fulfilled and the burden of giving it is shared.

Problem 5: Manipulation. Although most children can manipulate their parents to some degree, the circle's brand of parental manipulation is often difficult to discern because it is *subtle* and *indirect*. Circles hedge around the bush; they may whine or beg. Some will play a trade-off game: "I did this for you, why won't you let me do __?"

Solution: Make the *rules* clear from the beginning. Stick to them. Do not allow the emotions and personality of the circle to persuade you to bend the rules. If you do it once, you are putting yourself in jeopardy in the future. Also remember the circle's need to please. This child may capitulate if he/she sees that the *parent is displeased* with his/her behavior. This show of displeasure is often all that is required for a young circular child.

What to Expect from a Circle Child at Home

1. Lots of open affection. Circles give what they need.
2. Cooperation and helpfulness.
3. Sharing of toys and possessions.
4. Need for attention.
5. Need to talk and share self.
6. Many visitors. Circles have multiple friends and playmates even in the early years.
7. Heavy television watching. This must be monitored.
8. Honesty. Circles do tell the truth, even to their own detriment.
9. Messy room, a result of inherent laziness.
10. Predictable habits and routines. Once you know your circle child, he/she is easy to predict.

How to Raise a Circle Child

1. Be sure to provide **siblings/playmates.**
2. Let the circle **baby-sit**—he/she loves helping and acting like a grown-up parent.
3. Buy many **dolls** and/or **stuffed animals.** These can take on human characteristics for your child.
4. Get the child involved in organized **youth groups** as early as possible; i.e. scouts, church, 4-H, FFA, etc.
5. Provide a **large bedroom.** This child will have many guests and sleep-over buddies.
6. Encourage **team sports** for a boy or girl. This is a good outlet for a circle child, because it allows group interaction and requires the physical exercise that circle's tend to neglect.
7. Establish firm expectations for **good grades.** The circle child will do it to please you, but if you don't show this pleasure, he/she will stop. The peer group is more important to the circle than school performance. Try to direct this child into a peer group that values good grades.
8. Live in a **family neighborhood.** Even if you are a single parent, this is very important for your circle child.
9. Guide this child into a **people-oriented career.** From the elementary school artwork of people's faces to an "A" in English, history, and psychology in high school, reinforce your child's interest in people. Help him/her to explore professions that will allow constant interaction with others. Accounting or engineering are *not* right for circles. (See the next chapter for a list of typical circle jobs.)

10. Prepare yourself to be a good **listener** for the thoughts and feelings of your circle child. He/she needs to talk about everything he/she is experiencing. Give both *quality and quantity time.*

Final Note: All this effort will pay dividends in the future when this circle child is willing to generously share his/her time with old mom and dad. The adult circle will never miss Christmas holidays with the family and you'll be thankful to see your grandchildren several times a year. These are the ways the circle child will repay you for the love and attention that he/she received from you in the formative years. It's well worth it!

Chapter 16

The Circle at Work

If you work with a circle, you are fortunate. The circle will do his/her best to ensure a pleasant work environment for all those involved. The major characteristics of the circle shape are: friendly, nurturing, persuasive, empathic, accommodating, stabilizing, and reflective. These traits are admirable in a co-worker or a boss.

The types of job functions that would be most suitable for a person with the above characteristics are as follows:

secretary	housewife
salesperson	historian
clergy	astrologer
waitress/clerk	boy/girl scout leader
human resource specialist	camp counselor
personnel analyst	teacher/professor
mental health professional	trainer/consultant
nurse/doctor	

Although people who are dominantly circles may hold positions in management and administration, they will tend to have difficulty in these positions. *True circles are not power-oriented* (as the triangle is). Circles are much more concerned with people. That's why they are most often found in the helping professions. It is the circles among us who have cared about the less fortunate and the downtrodden in the world. Historically, circles have made this a better world in which to live.

HOW CIRCLES HANDLE CONFLICT

Conflict among and between people is the worst nightmare for a circle. Thus, a world in disharmony is the one most disrupting and unpleasant situation that a circle faces in life. Whether the conflict is between co-workers, or between the the Soviets and Americans, the circle will worry about it.

If the circle finds him/herself in direct conflict with another person, he/she will suffer more than any of the other four shapes. It doesn't matter who is right or who is wrong. It is the conflict itself that is so unpleasant. *Circles take it personally!*

The first impulse of the circle is to avoid the conflict and hope it will go away. Circles tend to give others the benefit of the doubt and even make excuses for irrational behavior in others. However, circles won't avoid the conflict for very long because they want to resolve the problem and return to their preferred state of harmony. They also take pride in being instrumental in conflict resolution.

When the subject of the conflict or the people involved are important to the circle, he/she will rely on two approaches to deal with it: (1) accommodation and (2) compromise.

Accommodation: The circle will always be the first person to give in to the needs of others. Although this may make co-workers happy because they will usually get their way, it is not always the best choice for the circle to make.

The circle may accommodate the wishes of another to the detriment of (1) the department as a whole, (2) the best solution for the majority, or (3) bending the rules that apply to all, for the needs of one. Often, circles end up with a bigger problem than they started with when they accommodate one complainer and hurt others in the process.

If there is disagreement between the circle and a co-worker over the way in which something should be done, the circle will most often be the person to give in. This is a problem when it was the circle who was "right" in the first place. By giving in, the circle *loses the respect of co-workers* who are concerned more with the issue than the persons involved.

Accommodation leads the circle to *save the relationship rather than to solve the problem*. When the circle hears angry words, he/she focuses on the *emotion* rather than on the subject of the emotion. This is where the problem lies. Circles will do anything to alleviate the anger, even if it means giving up their own good idea or what they know is the right thing to do.

Ultimately, the circle not only loses the respect of co-workers, but also loses some degree of *self-respect*. This is the most harmful of all.

Compromise: Smarter circles will use compromise more than accommodation to resolve conflicts. At least, in this way, there is "something in it" for the circle. He/she can maintain his/her self-respect in the process.

Circles will describe compromise as a win/win solution to the problem. However, true to the circular nature, the win for the circle is likely to be smaller than the win for the opponent.

HOW TO WIN AN ARGUMENT WITH A CIRCLE

1. Obviously, This Is a Less Difficult Assignment with a Circle Than with Any Other Shape. The circle will be the first to give in when there is conflict. The biggest problem is that the circle often perceives disagreement as a personal affront. He/she is bound to react more emotionally than any other shape. You must be prepared to deal with the emotion of the situation. Even if you are right, you may end up being the bad guy merely because you hurt the circle's feelings. In order to avoid this, you too must work for a win/win solution to the problem. *Do not allow the circle to completely accommodate you.* You will pay for it in the end!

2. Point Out Early That the Two of You Are Adults and Can Agree to Disagree. Make it clear that the circle should not take it personally. In this way, you will help the circle to focus on the problem rather than on the relationship between the two of you.

3. Assure the Circle That Your Conversation Will Be Kept Confidential. The circle is always concerned about the feelings of others and would be horrified to know that others are taking sides in the argument. Additionally, it is hard for true circles to be confidential themselves, so they tend to believe the same of others.

In fact, you will do best to keep the argument confidential. If your position is not the popular one and you elect to involve other co-workers, you will surely lose! The circle will go with the majority and make the popular choice if pushed to the wall.

4. Arrange for the Argument to Transpire in a Private Place. This will eliminate the involvement of others. Circles are prone to bring in "witnesses" on their own behalf.

A social setting away from the workplace is ideal when in argument with a circle. Invite the circle to lunch. This is one of his/her favorite times of the day. He/she will be more relaxed and affable, and you will have a better chance of getting your point across in this setting.

5. Get an Early "Yes" From the Circle on Another Issue. If the circle sees that you and he/she can at least agree on one thing, then this increases your chances of success on the major issue.

6. Demonstrate How Your Solution to the Problem Will Please Others. This is very important to the circle. Also, indicate your willingness to share the credit for the final decision with the circle. This allows the circle to save face back at the office.

7. Keep the Discussion Focused on the Problem. Circles will often attempt to involve other issues and people. They often use what others think as evidence to support their own point of view. Stick to the immediate problem and keep others out of it!

8. **You May Have to Force an Open Discussion of the Problem.** The circle really dislikes open confrontation and will often attempt to diffuse it. Present the problem and express your desire to resolve it.

9. **Whatever Is Decided, Present a United Front Between the Two of You When You Return to the Office and Co-workers.** Remember, maintaining relationships is most important to circles, and you may live to do battle again with this person.

Final Note: Throughout this situation, keep in mind that one of the attributes of the circle is his/her ability to *persuade* others. Thus, your circular opponent may be more skilled in argument than you suspect! Your advantage will be the knowledge that the circle's persuasive strength lies in his/her ability to trigger the emotions of others. Avoid this, and you increase your chances of winning.

THE CIRCLE CO-WORKER

Although the circle co-worker will be a delightful person with whom to work most of the time, there are some inherent problems that you should be aware of. These problems are a direct result of the *negative traits* of the circular shape, as follows: overpersonal, melancholic, manipulative, gossipy, self-blaming, apolitical, indecisive, and lazy. When the negative side of the circle emerges in the office, the following problems result.

Problem 1: "I can't work with someone I don't respect!" This is a lie. The circle really means "I don't want to work with someone I think doesn't like me!" (Circles often use the word *respect*, when it is really *being liked* that is important to them.)

Solution: Respond to the unspoken message. Give examples of past situations which demonstrate that the co-worker really does "like" the circle. Make it clear that this is not the issue.

Problem 2: "I'll have to check with Sam on this one." It is difficult for a circle to make a decision without knowing that others support it. Consensual validation is important to circles.

Solution: Check with others *before* bringing the problem to a circle. Be sure that the others support your proposal. This will both please the circle and demonstrate how much you think like he/she does. Be prepared for the circle to go back and check again before making the decision, however.

Problem 3: "I can't do everybody's work and mine too!" This is a common statement from circles. The reason is simple: they try to please people and often get in over their heads. Circles have trouble saying "no." When they have taken on too much, they begin to resent it and complain. However, they are their own worst enemies in this regard.

Solution: Help the circle to understand his/her own job responsibilities. Prioritize his/her work carefully. Do not allow him/her to take on the work of others. Monitor the amount of work being done. A circle does best working for one boss, not several.

Problem 4: "Let's take a break . . . ." Circles socialize and like to talk things over. They are good communicators and sense this strength. However, they are often found talking instead of working, and this can cause problems in an office. *Note*: This is particularly true if the circle is undergoing some personal life problems. He/she will take frequent breaks, make personal phone calls, and often be late to work.

Solution: Be sensitive to the circle's personal needs, but make it clear that you are not his/her "mother." A circle with a problem can monopolize your time. You have a job to do too. Be nice about it, but do not allow this to happen.

Problem 5: "Can you keep something to yourself?" This is the logical entry into the circle's breaking a confidence. Of all five shapes, the circle is the most prone to be gossipy. Although the information about someone else may be interesting, you must realize that tomorrow the gossip may be about you!

Solution: Do not tell a circle anything that you would not want others to know about you. You must share some personal data so that the circle will trust you, but monitor what you share.

Note: It is valuable to have a circle or two on your side if your company is highly political. The circles often tap into the informal networks. These grapevines are often useful in explaining the political inner workings of the company. However, realize that not all of the information is accurate. You will have to separate the valid from the "good story."

Problem 6: "I just didn't have time to get to it." One of the negative traits of the circular shape is *laziness*. It is often hard to pin down because the circle is such a skillful communicator; he/she will give you a hundred reasons why the job didn't get done!

Solution: Again, careful prioritization of the circle's work will solve this one. Get a commitment up front from the circle of how much he/she can accomplish in a given time period. Then, hold him/her to it!

Problem 7: "It's all my fault!" This is one of the toughest ones to deal with. The circle is *self-blaming* when things go wrong and he/she is found out. Although it is good that the circle is able to admit the wrong-doing, he/she has a tendency to overdo it, to the point of martyrdom!

Solution: Make the circle own up to the mistake, apply the proper discipline, then, forget it. Act like nothing happened and make it business as usual. You must show that it doesn't bother you or cause you to think less of the circle.

THE CIRCLE BOSS

Circles are perfectly capable of being effective managers of people. They possess some excellent attributes for this task. They are superb communicators and have a "sixth sense" about people. They are particularly effective as bosses in organizations that are *not* status- and rank-oriented. Circles truly believe in playing on the *team*. As bosses, they are sensitive to the needs of their employees and capable of using modern management techniques such as *participative management, quality circles,* and *matrix management.* However, as with all the shapes, there are pluses and minuses to the circular boss.

Pluses

1. Gives you a second chance . . . . a third, a fourth, etc. The circle believes in people!
2. Involves employees in decision-making.
3. Listens with concern to problems; is stabilizing.
4. Truly believes in the team management approach.
5. Highly persuasive and motivating.
6. Encourages social activities along with work.

Minuses

1. Has trouble disciplining and firing employees.
2. Slow decision-maker, lacks courage of his/her convictions.
3. Difficulty making unpopular decisions.
4. Weak political player.
5. Breaks confidences from one employee to another.
6. Uncomfortable with authority; sees self as a team player, not the coach!

How to Please a Circle Boss (and Protect Yourself in the Process)

1. **Be Prepared to Stop What You're Doing and Chat.** The circle likes to talk and prides him/herself on knowing the employees as people. Circle bosses have an **open-door** policy (which means *your door* must always be open to them).

2. **Be Willing to Share Personal Life Data.** Circles must *trust you as a person* to work with you effectively.

3. **Expect Lots of Meetings.** Circle bosses like to have all their people around them as much as possible.

4. **Do Not Lie to a Circle Boss or Break a Confidence.** Although he/she may do this to you, you are in the subordinate position.

5. **Readily Admit Errors and Mistakes.** Circles love to forgive, but they don't like to be lied to. In fact, you might think of your stint under a circular boss as a good opportunity to experiment. Take on that difficult assignment, take a risk! The circle boss will allow you to make mistakes where other bosses will not.

6. **Share Credit.** The circle boss wants to see that you are a good team-player and that you value your teammates.

7. **Refer to Your Circle Boss as Your Friend, Colleague, Mentor, etc.** When introducing him/her, say that you work together and, you may call him/her by his/her first name.

8. **However, Do Not Make the Mistake and Challenge the Authority of the Boss in Front of Higher Management.** You are still expected to treat your *friend* as the boss. Don't forget this. If there is conflict, the boss is still the boss!

9. **Don't Expect Quick Decisions.** The circle boss tends to waffle and will check with everyone before deciding. You will have a greater chance for success if you are the natural leader of your employee group. Present your proposal as a group proposal.

10. **Develop Social Expertise.** Don't miss an office party! To many circles, your attendance is a validation of their leadership ability. It's more important to attend the party than to be on time to work the next day.

Final Note: Relax! Circles do not like people who are uptight or trouble-makers. Circles don't like to be challenged. They like to maintain the status quo; they are *stabilizers*. Remember, "We're one big happy family around here!"

What You Will Learn Under a Circle Boss

1. The true meaning of **team play.**
2. The value of **collaboration** in problem-solving.
3. **Participative management** *does* work!
4. The value of a **mentor** who truly puts your development before his/her own advancement. (Note: Many circle bosses are used by upper management as *training managers*—people are assigned to their unit because they will take the time to train them well.)
5. The importance of a good **role model** to your future development and advancement into management.
6. The ability to **learn** and to **grow** in your chosen field under the guidance of an excellent teacher.

THE CIRCLE CUSTOMER

How to Identify a Circle Customer

1. You will instantly like this one! If you are going to be successful in the sale, you've got to make him/her like you too!

2. You may recognize this one, circles are the loyal customers and tend to bring return business.

3. The circle will be dressed in casual clothing with a pleasant smile and warm facial expression.

4. This customer is rarely alone. There are friends and/or family in tow.

5. The first contact is often initiated by the circle. There will be a big smile and a warm handshake.

6. The circle customer is not hurried. Shopping is a social event, like everything else.

7. The circle is often shopping on behalf of a friend or looking for a gift for someone.

8. During the sale, the circle may stop to greet friends or passers-by.

9. Expect this customer to ask you questions about *you* as much as about the product/service.

10. Don't expect an instant sale, the circle has to go home and check with others before buying.

How to "Sell" the Circle Customer

1. Make him/her like you; a circle might buy it just because he/she likes *you*.

2. Give full attention and show interest in him/her as a person.

3. Demonstrate that you, yourself, also use this product/service. This is very persuasive for a circle.

4. No hard sell! Casually mention price and features in the conversation.

5. Feel free to ask probing, personal questions. The circle loves to reveal self, and this may help you build an argument for your product/service.

6. Describe how popular your product is with others.

7. Do *not* criticize other competing products/services.

8. If possible, demonstrate how your product/service can be enjoyed in a social setting by several people at once.

9. Make the customer comfortable; bring coffee/soda.

10. If you make the sale, be sure to make a follow-up call. Circles love it!

Final note: If the circle customer is coming to you with a complaint, listen very carefully to what he/she has to say. Circles rarely complain and, when they do, it's serious. Do not take it lightly; and do something to correct it. If you make it right, the circle will be your customer for life!

Chapter 17

The Circle Under Stress

The circle and the box shapes share one important quality in common, they are both "Type B" personalities. This is very important when it comes to stress, because these two types are the ones who are least likely to feel stressed. This does not mean that they do not experience stress, it means that they are least likely to show it. "Type B's" are easy-going people who tend to take life as it comes. They are the stable ones.

Thus, if you are in a position where you work or live with a circle, this chapter is very important for you. You may be the person to first recognize it when your circle experiences a stressful situation in life. You need to know what to expect from your circle and how to best assist him/her in dealing with his/her difficult period.

How to Identify a Circle Under Stress

1. **Short-tempered.** Although the circle is naturally a bit moody, he/she is rarely abrupt with people. When this happens, you know something is wrong.

2. **Sullen/quiet.** This is unusual for the talkative circle.

3. **Poor Listener.** Active listening is one of the circle's strong traits. When the circle seems distracted in conversation, this is a warning sign.

4. **Withdrawal from People.** People and relationships are the "life blood" of the circle. This is a strong indicator.

5. **Preoccupied with Self.** Since circles place more emphasis on others than they do themselves, this indicates a problem. Circles rarely monopolize conversations with information about themselves.

6. **Insomnia.** Because the circle doesn't get enough daily exercise, this is a natural problem area.

7. **Daytime Fatigue.** Highly unusual for circles who try their best to always be "up" and happy for others.

8. Cancels Social Events. Never done by a normal, happy circle. He/she wouldn't miss a party.

9. Closed Door. Circle's doors are always open, welcoming visitors. This is an indicator of withdrawal.

10. Late to Work. Circles are usually early. They truly enjoy the camaraderie of the workplace.

Sources of Stress for Circles

I am dividing this section into two categories; (1) stress caused by the **home** environment and (2) stress experienced at **work**. Although the latter can be trying on a circle, stress in the home is the worst! *The home is the circle's refuge.* It must be smooth and stable. If there are problems at home, the circle will surely react in a negative manner.

Stressors at Home

1. Conflict Between Family Members. Family is the number one source of stress for a circle. The circle works hard at maintaining harmony in the home. When the harmony is broken, the circle will suffer more than the family members who are causing the conflict.

2. Trouble with Spouse. Of course, divorce is the very worst thing that can happen to the long-suffering, supportive circle. It is very rare for circles to get divorced and even rarer for them to initiate it. At the slightest ripple of difficulty, the circle will work hard to correct the perceived problem. He/she is usually successful, but suffers pain in the process.

3. Unruly Children Cause Stress for Circles. This is a fairly common occurrence in the life of a circle, because the circular parent is not a strong disciplinarian. For this reason, it is quite easy for the child to take advantage of the parent to get his/her way.

4. Disrupted Friendship Is More Stressful for the Circle in the Relationship Than It Is for the Other Party. Circles place great value on being a good friend. When they are not perceived as such, this is a stressful experience for them. *Note*: If the circle is the cause of the disruption, it is probably because he/she has betrayed a confidence.

5. Illness/Injury/Death of Loved One. Actually, the illness or injury of a loved one is not as stressful to the circle as it is to some other shapes. The reason is that these situations provide the circle with the opportunity to exercise his/her *nurturing* quality. However, when someone very close to a circle passes away, it is literally *devastating* to that circle. He/she feels deserted. It is not uncommon for circles to seek psychiatric help over the loss of a loved one.

If a circle listed the most stressful events that could occur in his/her life (in order of importance), the list would probably look like this:

1. Death of child
2. Death of husband/parent/sibling
3. Divorce/desertion
4. Death of friend
5. Serious illness/injury of loved one
6. Marital conflict
7. Conflict with child
8. Child leaving home
9. Conflict with parent/sibling/friend
10. Conflict between loved ones
11. Moving to a new home (leaving old friends)

Each of the above situations is more stressful to a circle than any work-related stress. Home is more important than office.

Stress at Work

Although problems at work take a backseat to home problems for the circle, there are some situations that can cause some minor stress. Even these diminish in importance if the circle has a harmonious homelife to return to after a stressful day at the office.

1. **Disagreement with Co-worker/Colleague/Boss.** Whatever the disagreement, it is more unpleasant for the circle involved since circles strive for harmony at work, as well as home. They try to make everyone at the office their friends. When someone doesn't accept this role with glee, the circle is disappointed and chagrined. It is important for circles to learn that they don't have to be everyone's friend to work with them.

2. **Office Isolation.** Circles need people around. If the circle finds him/herself in the back office, stuck away from everyone else, he/she will be unhappy. Circles like to be out on the floor dealing with people all day. They will even accept an assignment to be the customer service representative in charge of customer complaints, just to be with people!

3. **Undervalued in the Job.** Although the circle tends not to be an ambitious person, everyone needs to feel valued and worthwhile doing the job to which they are assigned. The circle is no exception. And . . . . a few "atta boys/girls" go a long way with a circle employee. They try to please.

Stressful People for Circles

1. **Boxes Are Number One!** The reason is simple; boxes are unemotional, cool, and aloof. They prefer not to mix business with pleasure. Boxes couldn't care less if people like them or not; they want respect, not love.

In this way, the box is the opposite of the circle. Circles often spend vast amounts of effort trying to reach box co-workers and turn them into friends. They rarely succeed. When the circle fails to make a friend of the box, he/she feels resentful toward him/her, or blames him/herself for the failure. Either way, it is a stressful experience for the circle.

2. Triangles Come in a Close Second. The true triangle is people-oriented only to the degree that people can help him/her. The triangle uses people for his/her own purposes, and this is thoroughly despicable in the eyes of the circle.

Historically, many circles have been used by triangles to "squeal" on others. The circle collects personal data about co-workers. People tell him/her things which they do not reveal to the untrustworthy triangle. All the triangle needs to do is to tap into the circle's database to find out the latest gossip. When the circle discovers that he/she has been betrayed, he/she becomes more wary of triangles in the future.

The remaining shapes—the squiggle and the rectangle—are no problem for circles. The circle is the most tolerant of human differences, so the squiggle's eccentric behavior doesn't bother the circle at all. The "confused" rectangle is a delight, because this person gives the circle the opportunity to help, nurture, and guide someone less sure than him-/herself.

Boxes and triangles, however, are the stressful people to circles. If the workplace is dominated by them, the circle must adapt to the situation and is rarely completely happy at work.

If the circle is married to a box or a triangle, some adjustment is required on the part of both spouses. The box spouse must learn to be more open and expressive of his/her feelings. The triangular spouse must bridle his/her need to dominate and must learn to compromise on decisions at home. If these actions are taken, a marriage between a circle and a box or a circle and a triangle can succeed. But it may be rough going in the early days of the relationship.

How the Circle Deals with Stress

1. Self-blame. When the circle is feeling stressed, his/her first impulse is to place the blame squarely upon his/her own shoulders. This is the anger stage turned inward. Circles are subjective in their approach to problem-solving.

2. Self-punishment. This is the "martyr syndrome" for which the circle is famous. Typically, the circle's punishment of self is not terribly severe. They merely *stay home from the party* and sulk alot. However, it should be noted that if the circle feels guilty enough, he/she is capable of doing bodily

harm to him/herself. Those close enough (friends/family) should monitor the circle's behavior under stress. Some circles have a history of hurting themselves. They may *overeat, fast,* or *drink too much.*

3. Plagues Others with Problem. This is very common behavior for the circle who needs to talk about everything, anyway. When the circle feels stress, he/she will talk to others incessantly about it. After hearing the "ain't it awfuls" day after day, this habit begins to wear thin for those who must listen to it. When the source of listeners dries up, the unhappy circle will seek out new ears. Rarely does this behavior solve the problem, but it certainly does make the circle feel better about it.

4. Withdrawal. This is usually the last stage of stress for the circle. When a circle becomes extremely melancholy, the bottom of the barrel has been reached. He/she will withdraw from everyone. This is the time to seek professional help for the stressed circle. He/she can no longer cope alone.

How to Help Your Circle to Reduce Stress

1. Be a Good Listener. Circles must have sounding boards. As long as the circle can talk about it, he/she is going to be OK.

2. Offer Objective Advice. Circles tend to be overly emotional and subjective. They need the balance of a coolly rational friend.

3. Prevent Self-punishment. Point out that this will not solve anything; it will merely make matters worse.

4. Stay Close. Call often and stop by to check on the circle. Be available for the 3 A.M. call to come in.

5. Encourage the Circle to Express Anger. This is difficult for circles, because they want everything to be pleasant and they don't want to offend others; but, this is a necessary stage that one must pass through when experiencing stress.

6. Insist on Physical Exercise. Circles tend to ignore this anyway, and they need it most when under stress.

7. Reinforce Positive Qualities of the Circle. Circles tend to really "get down" on themselves. They need propping up during this period.

8. Seek Professional Advice if the Circle Begins to Withdraw from You and Others. This is definitely a danger sign.

Remember . . . . your love and support for a circle during a stressful period will be repaid to you many times over. One of the circle traits is *generosity.* When the stress has passed, your circle will continue to repay you for years to come. You cannot find a better friend than a circle . . . . in good times and bad.

Circles feel most comfortable when . . . .

1. The "waters are smooth" at home and at work.
2. The circle is the center of a loving, happy family.
3. There are many close friends and/or relatives.
4. Our world is at peace.
5. The crime rate and unemployment are low.
6. Our leaders are fair and responsive to the less fortunate.
7. The high school reunion is coming up.
8. It's Christmas season and there are lots of gifts for all.
9. All the family is coming home for the holidays.
10. Everyone loves our special lover—our circle!

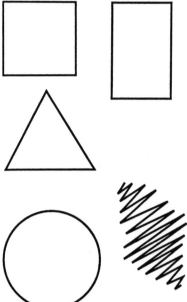

Section Five

THE FLIGHTY SQUIGGLE

Chapter 18

Identifying the Squiggle . . . .
_____ Catch Him if You Can!

Belief: "The world is a complex and exciting place to live in. There is always something to learn and to become."

Translation: "I still haven't figured out what I want to be when I grow up. With any luck, I never will."

You squiggles are like chameleons; you are constantly changing and accepting new challenges. I am very pleased that you have bought this book and are actually reading it! This is unusual for a squiggle. Good for you! It is common for squiggles to buy books on new and exciting topics but unusual for them to read the books. They tend to get bored very easily, put the book down, and move on to something else.

However, if you will "hang in there," I believe you will learn some interesting things about yourself. I will attempt to present this section in an exciting, fast-moving, succinct fashion to hold your interest. If you get bored along the way, please remember that other shapes are reading it, too, because they need to understand YOU! And . . . . that's not always easy to do.

OVERVIEW

"What if? . . . ." says the squiggle. This person is constantly thinking up new schemes. This is the most _right-brained_ person among us. This means that this individual does not process information in a logical, linear fashion. Instead, this person is **creative, conceptual, and intuitive** in the processing of information. The squiggle is most directly the opposite of the box. Squiggles are not detail-oriented people. They can do it if they have to, but they are basically very disorganized people. They are interested in *ideas*, not in the more practical matters of living. Both at work and at home, things just seem to fall through the cracks with a squiggle around. They are very weak in follow-up. It's not that they intend to forget, they just don't think that way!

Squiggles are **futuristic** in their life perspective. They are turned on by anything new and different in life. For this reason, others often perceive them as being unrealistic and rather ivory towerish in their approach to life.

Personality-wise, the squiggle is a pure delight. This person is naturally **expressive** and always excited about something. He/she is very **motivating** to others. At parties, the squiggle is **witty** and **sensuous,** again appealing to others.

QUICK INDICATORS OF SQUIGGLE PEOPLE

Language

Common Words: why? what if? idea, experiment, try, challenge, incredible, inconceivable, create, develop, begin, GO! and . . . . superlatives of all types.

Common Sayings: "I don't take NO for an answer!" "Paperwork is a waste of time." "He hasn't had an original idea in years!" "Why can't you see what is as clear as the nose on your face?" "This is the greatest!" "Wait 'til you hear this one!" "I've got the best idea of all!"

Appearance

Men: Casual, to the point of disheveled. Squiggles often look like they just got out of bed! They place no importance on appearance because physical, tangible things are never as important as ideas. The squiggle's profession will often dictate his manner of dress. For example, a university professor who comes to the office in a mixture of stripes and plaids may claim to be color-blind to cover his lack of awareness of dress. The classic squiggle engineer—who dresses in green polyester pants with outdated white belt, socks, and shoes and the wrinkled short-sleeved white shirt—is another example. Of course, you can't miss the ink stain in the shirt pocket from the felt tip pen left open or the 1958 briefcase that he wouldn't dream of parting with.

Of course the more theatrical types who are squiggles are much more fashion conscious. Their problem is overdoing it. They may emulate the

Don Johnson "Miami Vice" look at the banker's meeting. Or, the more dramatic squiggle may wear lots of gold chains hanging under his silk shirt that is unbuttoned down to his navel. Of course, the big diamond ring appears also.

Women: There is quite a variety here, but if the female squiggle had her way, she would be in her comfy, time-worn blue jeans with a T-shirt on that has her latest cause emblazoned across the front: "Save the Whales" . . . . "Save the Ozone".

Unfortunately, the squiggle can't wear this to work. She opts for comfort in the workplace. Prone to wearing loose-fitting clothing, the squiggle woman is found in the long flowing skirt with a blouse of comfortable, nondescript style. Those more artistic squiggles will tend to dress flamboyantly with bright colors and the latest fad from *Cosmopolitan* or MTV. It is not beyond reason for a squiggle to dress "punk" in the evening—to the point of purple hair and black leather.

Interestingly, I have noticed that squiggle women tend to be either *very fat* or *very thin*. Those with heavier body shapes will cover the bulk with large, dark, long jackets. The skinnies can wear anything, and they usually do.

Office

The squiggle office looks like a hurricane hit it! Papers are strewn everywhere . . . . the phone is ringing off the hook . . . . people are racing in and out; and the squiggle **loves** it that way. There must be lots of stimulating variety in this person's life, and the office reflects this. Of course, to the owner, it is all very organized and he/she can tell you exactly what is in every pile. To an outsider it is a sloppy, slovenly mess.

Squiggles work with manila file folders. They prefer these, because they are easily disposable. On occasion, squiggles are forced to use the more elaborate hanging style of "Pentel" folders. Invariably, when he/she takes them home at times, he/she snags a sweater on the metal clamp ends. Of course, this is of little concern to the squiggle, it's only clothing.

In terms of decorations, the squiggle's office is quite bleak. There are no family pictures (unless a concerned spouse brought one and planted it on the dusty shelf). For the more artistic squiggles, there might be a poster from the latest Agam art exhibit, maybe even a Keith Haring "inflated baby" cartoon character lying over behind the swivel chair.

In the extreme, there could be unopened packages and mail stashed in desk drawers waiting until the critical project is completed. Squiggle offices have been known to contain last night's late night dinner containers.

Cleaning people often refuse to clean this office, allowing it to go from bad to worse. However, this doesn't phase the squiggle who can be found working late, thinking "great thoughts" to the sound of his/her favorite classical music, or perhaps some jazz or new age music instead.

Personal Habits

1. **Fast Mover.** The classic squiggle is always in a hurry. He/she literally runs down the corridors, sometimes knocking people over. He/she doesn't stop to greet co-workers. This person is lost in thinking great thoughts.

2. **Interrupts. Doesn't Listen.** This is the major complaint of friends and associates of squiggles. The reason for this behavior is not ego-centric, it is idea-centric. The squiggle just can't wait to tell you his/her idea.

3. **Loses Things.** Because the squiggle is so scattered and disorganized, he/she is forever forgetting where something was put. I once saw a squiggle friend make a U-turn on the Interstate in rush-hour traffic to go home and get the manila folder of important papers for his 8 A.M. meeting. Not only was he late to the meetings (as usual), but the folder was sitting in his office the whole time.

4. **Daydreams Constantly.** Squiggles are forever fantasizing about everything. To the squiggle, life has no boundaries. The ability of the mind to conjure is unlimited. Walter Mitty must have been a squiggle!

5. **Stimulation-Seeker.** The squiggle needs constant stimulation, both professionally and personally. He/she seeks new situations, new people, new projects, new activities. I have known some radical squiggles who have shed jobs and wives at the same time. Unfortunately, many find that the grass is not always greener, but they keep jumping to the next meadow just the same.

6. **Rebel.** The squiggle likes to think of him/herself as different from others—as unique. The worst thing you can do to a squiggle is call him/her *average* or *normal*. Some squiggles will go out of their way to demonstrate this by taking up controversial causes. I've known union stewards and executives alike who were squiggles and referred to themselves as "rebels."

7. **Works Alone.** Particularly when the squiggle is involved in a new project that he/she is excited about, he/she can become very **intense** about it and puts in long hours alone. Because the squiggle is highly volatile, he/she does not function very effectively as a team member. If the team accepts his/her ideas, all good and well, but, if not—or if the project is boring—the squiggle would prefer to work alone.

8. **"Life of the Party."** Because of the natural wit of the squiggle, he/she can come alive in the social setting. At company parties, the squiggle who has been locked in his/her office brooding over that project for weeks

becomes the Life of the Party. Co-workers see a Jekyl-Hyde personality emerge.

9. **Doesn't Know a Stranger.** Squiggles are not particularly into people, like circles are. However, they are spontaneous and will talk to anyone about anything, particularly if the other person is willing to *listen* to them. In the bar, it is hard to tell the difference between the squiggles and circles. The exception is that the circles are listening, the squiggles are talking.

10. **Total Spontaneity.** The squiggle says exactly what comes to his/ her mind. He/she may ask embarrassing questions. However, since co-workers learn that this is a natural part of the squiggle personality, they tend to forgive any embarrassment the squiggle may cause. Also, co-workers often agree with what the squiggle says, but don't have the courage to say it themselves.

Body Language

1. **Quick, Fluid Body Movement.** The squiggle is not jerky like the rectangle, or slow and smooth like the triangle. He/she is fast and sure with movement reflecting clear purpose.

2. **Mercurial Facial Expression.** The face changes expression constantly. In a nanosecond, a wide grin appears over a new idea, then changes to a look of solemn concentration to unravel an intricate problem.

3. **Ubiquitous Eye Contact.** The squiggle's eyes are always flitting around and seem to be everywhere at the same time. Even when in one-to-one conversation, the squiggle seems to have trouble concentrating on you. However, he/she can also drift into a blank stare as the brain synapses fire. If the "eyes are the window of the mind," this is a dead give-away for the squiggle.

4. **Highly Animated Gestures.** Squiggles are always throwing their arms around and can go through ten different body postures within the first minute of a conversation. It's like watching a contortionist in front of your very eyes; entertaining to some, distracting to others.

5. **Voice Variety.** Another demonstration of the dramatic enthusiasm comes through the rich variation of the voice—the volume, rate, and pitch show constant changes in pattern.

6. **Constant Movement.** When the squiggle moves, the entire body moves synchronically. People often say that squiggles never stop moving, in fact. There is some part of their body that is always in movement— even in sleep!

7. **Nervous Tics.** If caught in a boring, structured, long-winded meeting, the squiggle will demonstrate his/her discomfort by strange, nervous twitches. There may also be audible foot shuffling or body position changing.

8. Sexual Cues. Some people interpret the squiggle's dramatic body expressiveness as sexuality. This is particularly true of open palm and arm gestures which function as "open invitations" to many.

9. High/Low Energy Deviations. This Jekyl/Hyde switching is conveyed overall through each of the expressions of the body. When experiencing intense concentration, the squiggle may not budge for hours on end. However, when people are around, the squiggle seems to be in constant movement.

10. Ectomorphic Body Shape. In my experience, most true squiggles are small, thin, wiry people. They can eat anything they want—at any time—and never gain weight. Their metabolism is the envy of everyone.

Final Note: Squiggles are the great *idea producers* of our society. They challenge the status quo. They force us to be more than we are today and more than we thought we ever could be. Without squiggles, we might still be in the Dark Ages.

Their personality traits are aligned with their strong right-brain dominance: **creative, intuitive, integrative, wholistic,** and **conceptual.** In interactions with others, they are highly **motivating, witty, persuasive,** and even **sexy!**

Squiggles must guard against their natural tendency to overpower others with their genuine **enthusiasm** and high **energy.** Others are often confused by the mercurial changes in the squiggle's temperament. Although the squiggle is usually positive and on what could be called "natural high," he/she can shift into intense concentration at a moment's notice. All behaviors are spontaneous.

The largest problem is living in this organized, highly logical and linear world. The squiggle often feels left out. Because he/she is not detail-oriented and highly methodical, this person often has trouble in organizations. A squiggle should never work in a bureaucratic, routine, structured job. He/she requires freedom and the ability to experience a multitude of varied stimuli on a daily basis. When properly challenged, the squiggle produces great ideas and contributes to society.

Chapter 19

The Squiggle at Home

If you live with a squiggle person, there is never a dull moment in your life. Squiggles are happiest when there is something new and exciting going on. And . . . . if there is nothing, the squiggle will create it! Squiggles *love change* and are drawn to the unusual, the unique. They are futuristic and are usually miles and years ahead of the rest of us in their thinking.

Because the squiggle is the most right-brained shape of the five, all of the creative characteristics abound within the squiggle.

In order to understand the squiggle better, it may be useful to point out that there are certain traits that the squiggle shares with each of the other shapes:

1. Triangles and Squiggles Share a Powerful Personality. However, the reasons for this are different. The triangle is self-centered and ambitious; the squiggle is an ardent salesperson for a new idea or concept.

2. Boxes and Squiggles Appear to Others as Loners. However, the squiggle gains the label of loner from his/her tendency to withdraw into his/her head (the world of ideas). The box withdraws into the office to get the work done.

3. Circles and Squiggles Share an Outward Moodiness of Personality. However, the reason for the mood changes is different. The circle becomes depressed over problems in relationships, where the squiggle could care less about what people think of him/her. The squiggle's moodiness comes from the flights of fantasy that run rampant within his/her head and the sudden crashes down to earth that everyday living causes. The squiggle personality ranges from extreme ecstasy over a great new idea to total silence and deep withdrawal when developing a new theory or analyzing a complex problem.

4. Rectangles and Squiggles, to the Outside Observer, Appear to Be the Most Alike, but They Are Not. Although the outward behavior of both

shapes is somewhat **erratic,** the reasons are different. As well as being in transition to a new state of being, the rectangle is confused about his/her position in life. The squiggle does that every day. Whereas the squiggle has a "method in his/her madness," the rectangle's behavior is unpredictable to both the outside world and to him/herself.

Thus, if you live with a squiggle and you are *not* a squiggle yourself, the explanation above may help you to understand why you and your squiggle share certain characteristics in common, but are very different in other ways. Remember, we all have the traits of all five shapes within us. Thus, each of us has certain traits that are dominant in another shape.

THE SQUIGGLE SPOUSE

How to Create an Ideal Squiggle Home

Variety is the spice of life for a squiggle. Thus, your home environment must reflect this. The suggestions below will assist you in accomplishing this.

1. **Every Room Should Have a Different Decor.** The same old thing is boring to a squiggle. You can mix wood with metal and glass, but do stay with **modern motif.** Remember, your squiggle is futuristic. (Be sure to include a geodesic dome.)

2. **Use Stimulating Colors for the Dramatic Squiggle.** Use reds and bright hues of orange, fuchsia, purple, etc. No pastels for this shape.

3. **Artwork and/or Sculpture Goes with Squiggles as They Tend to Be Artistic Themselves.** True squiggles will want whatever is the "latest." At the writing of this book, artists such as Julian Schnabel, David Salle, Keith Haring, or Brian Hunt would be appropriate. However, many squiggles of the '60s will prefer Lichtenstein, Warhol, Johns, Rauschenberg, or de Kooning. No glitsy black velvet Elvis portrait or cheap seascapes for the discriminating squiggle.

4. **Entertainment Options in the Home Will Please a Squiggle;** for example, a piano, computer, pool table, jacuzzi. Squiggles like lots of choices.

5. **Spacious Rooms Are Important.** Squiggles need "room to think." A private den area is also advisable. Squiggles need a place to escape and to enter the "reality of the mind."

6. **Reading Materials Should Abound.** Literature in the squiggle's professional interest and cutting edge periodicals (*Omni*, Naisbitt *Trend Letter*). There are often "new age" books such as *Crack in the Cosmic Egg, Out on a Limb* to satisfy the metaphysical side. Science fiction is also popular.

7. **Modern Appliances and Electronic Gadgets Are a Delight to Squiggles.** The more complex, the better. The squiggle will spend hours putting it together or figuring it out. (The triangle needs these things for status but never figures out how they work.)

8. **No Set Routines at Home for a Squiggle.** They like surprises. You may have a lovely dinner fixed and your squiggle comes home and says, "Turn the oven off, we're going out tonight!" *You have to be very flexible to live with a squiggle!*

9. **Squiggles Will Tend to Prefer a Small Family.** They are not particularly people-oriented and prefer to choose a small, select group of friends and acquaintances. The less they see of relatives, the better.

10. **Save Your Money, Because Your Squiggle Won't.** True squiggles are bored to death with monthly bills and routine financial commitments. They eschew the company retirement plan. Squiggles do like the gamble of speculative stocks and high-risk investments. Sometimes this can pay off big for squiggles.

Note: Of the five shapes, the *triangle and squiggle are most likely to become millionaires.* The triangle plots his/her course, while the squiggle often lucks into it. I would be willing to bet that there are more squiggle lottery winners than any of the other shapes. However, the squiggle can be a millionaire one day, and a pauper the next.

Recreation for the Squiggle

1. **Unusual Hobbies Are the Norm:** salt water tropical fish, miniature houses, metal sculpture, bombs, etc. If the squiggle likes pets, they will be unusual: a Russian wolfhound, miniature chihuahua, boa constrictor, you-name-it.

2. **You Will Enjoy Exciting Vacations with Your Squiggle Spouse.** Squiggles will choose the travel folder on the USSR, trekking through India, or the African safari. They may want to visit Belfast or Jerusalem during the height of battle.

3. **Squiggles Will Enjoy the Latest Movie if It Is on a Unique Topic.** They particularly enjoy science fiction, spy intrigues, and horror shows. Squiggles are the lifetime fans of the midnight *Rocky Horror Show*. No tear-jerkers, please.

4. **Small Gatherings or Wild Parties**—the squiggle enjoys both social settings. A squiggle can be found in the center of a group of intellectuals—happily discussing world peace—or at the huge outdoor concert yelling and screaming. It is just as likely that you can find a squiggle at home on Saturday night buried in a mountain of books.

5. Squiggles Are Avid Readers. Actually, the squiggle is happy to gain information from any source: books, television, people. It doesn't matter, as long as the squiggle is learning something new. The squiggle is a lifelong learner.

6. Unique Sports Would Be the Choice of Squiggles. They are not interested in team sports or in athletics in general. However, something like hot air ballooning or hand gliding holds appeal for the squiggle.

7. Very Few Squiggles Live Their Lives without Trying Their Hand at Poetry or Music. They may even have a history of amateur theatrics. These are natural outlets for the creative impulse of the squiggle.

8. If the Squiggle is a Collector, the Object of His/Her Affection May Seem a Little Weird. I have known squiggles to collect elephant ceramics, antique hat pins, juke boxes, '40s music, and Andy Warhol memorabilia.

9. Mind Games Are the Preference of Squiggles. Any game that will challenge the mind will do: bridge, I.Q. riddles, chess, *Pente*, *Scrabble* and crosswords of all sorts. The biggest problem the squiggle has is finding a worthy opponent.

10. Computers Are the Squiggle's Favorite Pastime. As a child, the squiggle goes from Atari and Nintendo to *Dungeons and Dragons*. As an adult, the squiggle prefers to develop his/her own software systems. It is very unusual to find a squiggle without at least one personal computer at home.

11. Squiggles Find Good Entertainment in Visiting Museums of All Sorts. They particularly like museums of science and industry, space, aeronautics, avionics and art. It is the squiggles who love the Epcot Center at Disneyworld. (Although they may not admit it, they enjoy the fantasy park as well.)

12. Last on the List of Recreational Preferences Is Family Activity (Except Having Sex, of Course). This is not the squiggle's strong suit. Things like reunions, and backyard barbecues turn off the squiggle, unless these events are done with great flair and originality. Squiggles tend to forget important dates such as birthdays and anniversaries. When reminded, they feel guilty, but they don't change. If you are married to a squiggle, don't expect gushing sentimentality or a surprise party for your 40th birthday. However, if you will remind him/her, there may be two tickets for a Mediterranean cruise on the kitchen table a week later.

Special Note: Of all five shapes, the squiggle is the least likely to be married and have a family. Squiggles often stay single throughout life, and/ or move in and out of many different relationships. They may have been married several different times. The more traditional squiggle who does not have a taste for divorce may satisfy his/her need for variety through extra-marital affairs.

What to Expect from Your Squiggle Spouse

Pluses

1. Constant unpredictable change.
2. Stimulation and exciting people.
3. High energy and animation.
4. Excellent sense of humor.
5. Sudden, unexpected successes.
6. Direct, honest responses (at the moment).
7. "Life of the Party" sociability.
8. Surprises—some good, some bad.
9. Creative intelligence.
10. Early "peaking." Squiggles are most creative early in life. Their greatest successes tend to occur then. Appreciate it while it's happening.

Minuses

1. Fickle in relationships.
2. No roots—constant movement of family to new places.
3. Erratic shifts from flamboyance to boredom.
4. Some big *failures* in life to match the successes.
5. Loneliness. Squiggles are often absent or mentally removed.
6. Few friends. Squiggles are not into being popular.
7. Lack of openly expressed affection.
8. Disorganization—too many balls in the air.
9. Sloppy personal habits.
10. Impatience with slower thinkers. Weak in the teaching function of parenting.

How to "Accentuate the Positive" in Your Squiggle

1. Keep a tight rein on the budget; discourage impulsive buying.
2. Force spouse to keep family commitments; use guilt if necessary.
3. Plan home events to keep your squiggle at home more (but be prepared to cancel at the last minute).
4. Show interest in your spouse's profession.
5. Get excited about his/her great new ideas, but realize they will change tomorrow.

6. Create some new ideas and excitement of your own. This keeps your squiggle interested in you.
7. Do not become sucked into the low moods; keep an even keel.
8. Be there for the failures. Rejuvenate your squiggle with past successes and courage to face the future. (The flipside of this one is to enjoy the successes.)

How to "Protect Yourself" in This Relationship

1. Avoid building expectations of how things should be. They never will be, or, when you get there, it will change.
2. Establish a clear delineation of "turf"—what belongs to whom.
3. Build some **permanence** into the family structure: save money, establish a residence, establish credit, plan for retirement.
4. Prepare yourself for idiosyncratic behaviors. Squiggles can get a little weird. Learn to say NO!
5. Establish a normal homelife for your children.
6. Develop your own personal support system of friends. Do not depend upon your squiggle for emotional support.
7. Pursue your own career; don't be dependent.
8. Prepare to play second fiddle at parties and (sometimes) to play chauffeur to a drunk on the way home.
9. Give love and support without expecting an equal amount in return.
10. Maintain your sense of humor. You'll need it!

HOW TO FIND A SQUIGGLE MATE

Places to Find Squiggles

1. In the supermarket at midnight.
2. Behind a terminal in a high tech company.
3. In a glider/sailboat/parachute.
4. In the science or art museum.
5. At the play/symphony/ballet.
6. Anywhere in a university.
7. In the stained glass window class.155001
8. Around the pool at the nudist camp.
9. At home reading a book.

What to Say to a Squiggle

1. "I've got a great idea!"
2. "I like the way you think."
3. "What are your predictions for the economy in 1990?"
4. "Do you agree with Carl Sagan about the ozone?"
5. "I must remember to renew my membership in the Futurist Society."
6. "Which one did you like best—*Close Encounters*, *Alien*, or the *2001* series?"
7. "What do you think of compact discs?"
8. "You're not like other men/women!" (Squiggles love to be perceived as unique.)

What to Do on the First Date

1. Wear a T-shirt that says "E.T. Lives!"
2. Go to a large party and enjoy the squiggle's performance.
3. Go to an art museum showing.
4. Take in a Buckminster Fuller lecture.
5. Create a mosaic at home.
6. Get "plastered" together on a bottle of ouzo.
7. Hop on a jet to Quebec or Bar Harbour, Maine.

How to Approach the "Sexual Question"

1. Use straight, pure seduction and make it *dramatic*! *Squiggles are the sexiest and most dramatic of the shapes*!

2. Go the whole nine yards. Men, wear bikini briefs, women wear the black and red garter belt.

3. A little "kink" may be desirable. You may want to go to a sex shop first for instrumentation. You might suggest involving others in later encounters.

4. A triple "X" movie will set the mood.

5. Get yourself in shape first. Squiggles tend to be long-lasting love makers.

6. *Be good*! Squiggles get bored easily.

7. If you do fall in love, don't plan on a lengthy courtship. A fast weekend to the coast and a justice of the peace is the squiggle's style.

8. Enjoy it! You've just managed to hook the most desirable sexual partner of the five shapes. Needless to say, you will not lack for stimulation

in this department in the future. The trick is to keep your squiggle partner interested from this point on. Remember, squiggles tend to be fickle.

THE SQUIGGLE CHILD

It is very important to point out right at the beginning of this section that *every pre-school age child acts like a squiggle!* This is the life stage in which the squiggle traits are most observable: creative, intuitive, naturally expressive, disorganized, unrealistic, illogical, uninhibited, and naive. One could actually say that the squiggle person is, in fact, child-like.

Thus, if you have a pre-schooler at home, do not be too quick to characterize him/her as a squiggle personality. When this child gets a bit older, you may observe the emergence of stronger box, triangle, or circle traits within him/her.

If your child is already in school and you are absolutely *sure* that you have a squiggle on your hands, the following are typical problems that you may face and the solutions may be valuable to you as a parent.

Problem 1: Low Marks in School. This is not unusual for a squiggle child, and the reason is that he/she becomes easily bored. This does not mean that your child is not intelligent. In fact, squiggles are often *very intelligent*. This is part of the problem—they lack challenge.

Solution: Have your child tested early for the gifted classes, which tend to be more challenging. Choose his/her teachers carefully to ensure high quality. Always get involved in the child's homework and reward good school performance at home.

Problem 2: Lack of Perseverance. Regardless of the task, if the squiggle is not challenged—or if the challenge is too great—this child will tend to give up!

Solution: Direct the child into activities which are appropriate for his/her level. Try to involve him/her with other children to accomplish the task. Group competition may keep him/her more interested for a longer period.

Problem 3: Destructive with Possessions. The creative personality wants to see how things work. This child may tear things apart, dissect or combine things just for experimentation. Once done, he/she doesn't like to have to put it back.

Solution: Buy creative toys and gifts: chemistry set, building blocks, astronomy kit, puzzles, etc. Do not buy breakable, fragile items.

Problem 4: Breaks the Rules. Even from an early age, the squiggle dislikes rules and structure. He/she hates set routines. This child does not want to be put "in a box." (*Note:* if you are a box parent, this will be difficult for you. This child is your opposite in this way.)

Solution: Insist on certain, necessary daily routines. Use punishment to ensure that they are followed, but do not suffocate this child with rules. Allow for creativity.

Problem 5: Normal Logic Doesn't Apply. This child is not swayed by logic. The squiggle is the least likely to respond to traditional values and beliefs. The squiggle won't do it just because "momma said so," or because "everyone in the neighborhood does it this way."

Solution: You'll have to learn to be more creative with your reasons why the child must do something. A squiggle child will respond favorably to a new idea or game. If you can think of a way to make a game out of the task, you will be more successful. However, you must be firm in insisting that there are certain unacceptable behaviors. You must build in a respect for higher authority as well. The reason for this is the child's future. Squiggle children who grow up not able to respect authority have major problems in the workplace dealing with bosses.

Problem 6: Manipulation. The circle child manipulates by whining, the triangle by bargaining. The squiggle manipulates by the sheer force of argument. Squiggles believe strongly in their own ideas. They have the charismatic skills to persuade others to their point of view. (This is why evangelical preachers are listed as squiggles.)

Solution: Keep your logical, left-brain functioning as you listen to the latest request of your squiggle. Do not allow yourself to be swayed by his/her dramatic presentation.

What to Expect from the Squiggle Child at Home

1. Messy room
2. Lost or broken possessions
3. Forgetful of rules/commitments
4. Positive attitude
5. High energy—can seem "hyper"
6. Short attention span
7. Multiple hobbies/interests
8. A few close friends (they may be weird)
9. Enthusiasm versus boredom, changes instantly
10. Intuitive, "sixth sense" about people and situations (Note: Squiggles have been known to be clairvoyant.)

How to Raise a Squiggle Child

1. Be firm in setting and enforcing rules for home tasks and personal behavior.

2. Allow mistakes. This is critical to support a creative personality.

3. Lower your own expectations about your child being the girl/boy next door type. This is no typical child. Do not compare him/her to others.

4. Be sure to locate an appropriate school situation for this child. If he/she is properly challenged, he/she can excel! The intelligence is there.

5. Encourage friends and playmates. The squiggle has so much going on in his/her own little world, that he/she may appear to be anti-social. Reinforce the value of people in life.

6. Involve the squiggle child in group activities. Involvement in sports is excellent. This is important because he/she can easily become a "wimp-type" egghead.

7. Stick to a pre-determined weekly allowance. Squiggles are not strong in money matters. They tend to be impulsive buyers. Do not buy the child everything he/she wants. Teach discretion.

Final Note: The squiggle child is a dreamer. He/she can get lost in the fantasy world of his/her mind. Ask him/her to share these dreams with you. Some will be crazy and off the wall. Others are possible. Reinforce those dreams because *your support can make a difference in your child's life.* Remember, squiggles often make their dreams come true!

Chapter 20

The Squiggle at Work

It is completely possible for a squiggle to function normally and happily in the right job. However, if the squiggle is misplaced and asked to perform routine, mundane work in a highly structured organization, there definitely will be a problem. Squiggles need excitement and variety in every aspect of their lives. They need the type of job in which they have the freedom to explore and to experience a variety of people and types of tasks.

Of course, over time and with age, the squiggle will adapt to the needs of his/her environment. He/she may have to perform a routine job during the day, but after 5 P.M., watch out! You can find your squiggle in every after work bar in town. He/she may even own one. (Squiggles often moonlight in their preferred line of work.) If his/her need for excitement is not filled during the workday, he/she will find a way to satisfy it after work.

However, if the squiggle is appropriately placed in a job function that challenges his/her innate abilities, the creative energy will be released to the benefit of the employer. Below is the list of jobs for which squiggles are the best suited:

strategic planner	chef
artist/performer/poet	new product specialist
musician	international sales/marketing
university professor	promoter/public relations
scientist/researcher	entrepreneur
artificial intelligence expert	real estate agent
astrologist	interior decorator
inventor	evangelical preacher

HOW SQUIGGLES HANDLE CONFLICT

If the subject of the conflict is unimportant to the squiggle, he/she will *avoid it* entirely. This method is chosen not for fear of offending a co-worker or colleague; it is the squiggle's choice because he/she has too many things to do—too many mountains to climb to get involved in some petty office disagreement. The problem is, when the squiggle refuses to get involved in the search for a solution to the problem, the group loses his/her valuable, creative ideas and input.

If the problem is an important one to the squiggle, and if he/she has strong views on how it should be solved, he/she will definitely get involved. In fact, next to the triangle, the squiggle is the *most competitive shape* of the five. Squiggles will compete with vigor when it is their idea that is at stake. And, they are often successful because of their strong *persuasive skills*.

If you are in the position of having to do battle with a squiggle, you will need all of your weapons at your service. In battle, the squiggle is as strong as the triangle; in some ways more so because the squiggle truly believes in what he/she is arguing for. The triangle often just wants to win for the sake of winning.

HOW TO WIN AN ARGUMENT WITH A SQUIGGLE

1. **First of All, You Must Steel Yourself Against Being Swayed by the Powerful Energy and Evangelistic Dogmatism of Your Opponent.** Squiggles often win arguments merely because their opponent is awe-struck by their strong presentation.

2. **Plan for Two Sessions.** Use the time in the first session just to *listen* intently to the squiggle's argument. Allow the squiggle to rant and rave and use up all of his/her polemic skills. Once he/she has performed this catharsis of feeling, he/she will be more open and able to listen to your side in the second session.

3. **Choose a Place to Hold the Discussion Outside of the Squiggle's Chaotic Office.** Try to persuade him/her to come to your office. This is ideal; it automatically gives you the psychological advantage. If the squiggle disagrees (which is likely), offer a neutral meeting place like a conference room or restaurant.

Combining your first session meeting with lunch is a good possibility if you are in control. Take the squiggle to your private club where only you can pay the bill. Order an expensive lunch (squiggles like anything flambé or foreign food, of course). Your strategy will be to limit the time you have for the lunch and delay discussion of the problem until the end. When the squiggle finishes expressing his/her side of the issue, leave abruptly for another meeting. This tactic will ensure a second session because agreement was not reached.

4. Let the Squiggle Win the First Round. If he/she leaves the first session feeling victorious, he/she will let his/her guard down for the second one. This will be to your advantage.

5. Allow Time to Pass Between the First and Second Sessions. The squiggle may change his/her mind or totally forget about it in the interim. Squiggles are weak in perseverance.

6. Turn the Tables on the Confident Squiggle in the Second Session. First, use the element of surprise; do not give the squiggle any warning. Merely appear on his/her doorstep, close the door, and demand a continuation of the lunch discussion.

7. Next, Make a Powerful Presentation on Behalf of Your Side of the Issue. This time you must be the one who is excited and absolutely immovable in your position. During your argument, demonstrate how the squiggle will benefit from adopting your solution.

8. If It Appears That You Are Losing the Battle, Quickly Change the Subject to Something More Remote. Squiggles are easily sidetracked. You might "pull rank" if you outrank the squiggle.

9. If You Seem to Be Winning, Move for Agreement on the Spot. Be sure to have all necessary papers, etc., with you so that they can be signed while the squiggle is in agreement. He/she may change his/her mind again momentarily.

10. If You Do Win the Altercation, Be Prepared to Do the Follow-up Work Yourself. This is not the strong suit of the squiggle. What squiggles agree to do one day, they often forget the next. You must be responsible for working out the details if the agreement is to be carried out.

If you don't win, crawl away, lick your wounds, and review this page for the next encounter. You are not the first (nor the last) to be beaten by a squiggle. This is a very formidable opponent.

THE SQUIGGLE CO-WORKER

The following list of typical problems encountered by co-workers of squiggles will be useful to you if you work directly with a squiggle. Suggested solutions are offered to deal with each of the problem areas.

Problem 1: "Why Can't You Understand . . . . A = A!" Squiggles become very *impatient* when co-workers don't understand them. The problem is magnified by the fact that co-workers often do not understand squiggles. They don't think logically and sequentially like the rest of the world does. They are the **new minority**—the right-brained minority!

Solution: You must deal with two problems here: (1) the emotional impatience of the squiggle and (2) communication problem between a left- and a right-brainer. First, do not feel stupid. Be calm; show him/her your desire to understand. Second, have the squiggle repeat it and ask questions that will quicken your understanding. You *can* understand a squiggle. The problem is that *they leave things out of their communication.* They jump to the end too quickly. You must make the squiggle fill in the blanks.

Problem 2: "Don't Say No Until You Hear Me Out!" Here we have the problem of the squiggle who wants it his/her way. Squiggles (like triangles) want it *their way* and will fight tenaciously to convince others. They have difficulty accepting a "no" answer when they believe strongly in their idea. They will continue to lambaste co-workers until they get agreement.

Solution: Squiggles need to learn that they cannot always have things their way when they live in organizations. Sit the squiggle down and point out the reasons why we cannot implement his/her idea right now. Compliment his/her thinking; do not squelch the creative impulse. Other ideas may have more merit.

Problem 3: "Paperwork Is a Waste of Time!" Squiggles do not adjust well to bureaucratic companies. They are not detail-oriented. They are idea-oriented. Your squiggle co-worker may try to pawn off his/her paperwork onto you.

Solution: This gets very old. Co-workers finally get enough of doing the squiggle's work for him/her. There are two solutions. The first is the most difficult, but worth the effort if there truly is too much paperwork in your company. Use the squiggle as an ally to reduce the amount of paperwork flow. Simplify forms, etc. Go to the boss with your proposal.

The second solution is merely to refuse to do the squiggle's work and let the chips fall where they may. You cannot allow the squiggle to continue to manipulate you. You have your share of work to complete also.

Problem 4: "Where Has He/She Gone Now?" Squiggles have a tendency to just disappear. They need time alone. They will often find an empty office to hide in or bury themselves in the stacks of the library. Regardless, they are often not there when you need them. They have little or no commitment to the team. The true squiggle is a *loner* and really doesn't care how others feel about him/her.

Solution: Squiggles must learn responsibility to others. They are part of the team, but do not see themselves as team players. It is probably necessary for management to intervene on this one. The boss must make it clear to the squiggle that he/she must be available to—and work effectively with—his/her co-workers for the team to function properly.

Problem 5: "Have You Heard the One about the $@#%*?" This problem is specific to male squiggles. They often have a "dirty mouth" in the office. Although the squiggle is known for his/her excellent sense of humor, this can grind upon co-workers if it is not done in good taste. Plus, squiggles are famous for interrupting others whenever they so choose.

Solution: Make it clear to your squiggle co-worker that those kinds of jokes offend you. You can also prevent this problem if you appear to be all business when you see the squiggle coming your way.

Final Note: Squiggles can cause chaos in a normal office setting if they are allowed to do as they please. This creative type actually has no business in a structured office. This is the province of boxes and the box and the squiggle are opposite personalities. The squiggle is best placed in more free-flowing, less structured job situations. The bureaucracy is not the place for the squiggle personality. (See job listings for squiggles.)

THE SQUIGGLE BOSS

Unfortunately, the squiggle boss is a contradiction in terms. Pure *squiggles should not be bosses*—at least not in highly structured organizations. They do not have the temperament or organizational skills for the job. The worst management job for a squiggle is middle management. The squiggle rebels against the chain of command. He/she has great difficulty implementing a policy that he/she does not believe in.

Ironically, if the squiggle is found in a management position, the best place for him/her is at the top of the hierarchy! At least as the company president, he/she can better use his/her motivational skills to implement new ideas. The squiggle executive can delegate the detail work that is his/her weakness. (This is why the squiggle is often successful as an *entrepreneur*.)

If you find yourself reporting to a squiggle boss, there are certain things you should know that will make your life easier. The situation is not hopeless, squiggles do have some excellent qualities needed for a position of authority.

Pluses

1. Spontaneous enthusiasm
2. Employees are given free rein
3. Loose rules
4. Receptive to any new idea
5. Nonjudgmental about people
6. Open, honest expression of feelings
7. Employees have a sense of equal status with boss
8. Boss is a great cheerleader (as long as it's being done his/her way)

Minuses

1. Disorganization
2. Lack of attention to detail
3. Erratic policy making
4. Constant changes
5. No follow-up
6. High absenteeism
7. Little performance feedback given
8. Naive to organizational politics

How to Please Your Squiggle Boss

1. Have a great new idea every day.
2. Get excited about whatever the boss says.
3. Be enthusiastic about your job.
4. Support your boss first, co-workers second.
5. Do not "play personalities."
6. Develop your own work schedule. Do not expect boss-imposed structure.
7. Be a self-starter.
8. Force the boss to give you a performance appraisal.
9. Keep notes on the contributions you have made.
10. Learn to avoid the boss during his/her intense periods of withdrawal.
11. Develop a fast wit to respond to that of the boss. (Do laugh at the boss's jokes.)
12. Develop good rapport with other department managers. You must keep your options open for upward movement.

Final Note: Do not expect to fair well under a squiggle boss if you are ambitious. The squiggle boss is not even concerned about his/her own advancement, let alone yours. This boss is a weak political player. You will have to ferret out the politics for yourself and manage your own career.

THE SQUIGGLE CUSTOMER

How to Identify a Squiggle Customer

1. The clothes either don't match or he/she looks like he/she slept in them. Squiggles are not concerned with their appearance. They tend to look sloppy and unkempt.

2. The squiggle customer may *look poor*, but isn't!

3. Body movements will be fast and jerky. The squiggle is always in a hurry. He/she will either avoid the handshake, or may shake your arm out of the socket!

4. Fast talker. Try to keep up. The squiggle's mind races and jumps from one question to the next.

5. Prepare to be interrupted in the middle of an answer with another question.

6. Quick assessment of you and your product/service. The squiggle mind is fast. He/she will do a quick scan of your operation.

7. Can appear to be momentarily distracted. This is when the squiggle has retreated into his/her head. A decision is being made.

8. The squiggle customer will make a quick, impulsive decision to buy, or not to buy. Once the decision is made, it will be impossible for you to overturn it. Don't try.

How to "Sell" a Squiggle Customer

1. Talk fast; the squiggle is impatient.

2. Crack a joke or two (make them good).

3. Demonstrate all the "bells and whistles"; squiggles love things that are complex.

4. Describe how your product/service is unique.

5. Explain how few customers can really appreciate the quality of what you are selling.

6. Compliment the squiggle's quick understanding.

7. Describe it as a "new, revolutionary" system, line, creation.

8. Tell about the genius who created your product/service.

9. Go for the sale quickly; this is an impulsive buyer. Cost is a minor factor if he/she wants it.

10. Go for the sale of any ancillary equipment or attachments. The squiggle is likely to buy the whole ball of wax.

Final Note: Be sure to carefully explain your company's *return policy*. The squiggle is famous for returning things which he/she purchased too impulsively. And . . . . the squiggle has no compunction about returning an inferior product. The circle will keep it because he/she doesn't want to hurt your feelings. The squiggle couldn't care less.

Chapter 21

_____ The Squiggle Under Stress

The squiggle is definitely a "Type A" personality and *happy about it*! The squiggle (like the triangle) is a **stimulation-seeker.** The squiggle has to have lots of things going on in his/her life to be happy. He/she cannot survive in a boring everyday rut in which everything happens today just as it happened yesterday. This is comforting to most people, but stressful to a squiggle.

Squiggles thrive on change. Doing it the same old way is totally boring. Squiggles never want to maintain the status quo; they want to try something new. The right brain of the creative squiggle is always working, fantasizing about new schemes. There is constant mental activity going on within the squiggle, even in sleep. Thus, change is the very lifeblood of the squiggle personality.

A squiggle's major source of stress is a routine, mundane, predictable life. When this happens, the squiggle will retreat to the inner recesses of the mind. It is important to understand that the squiggle has a different reality from most of us. *Reality is inner*; the outer semblances of life are fragmentary. The squiggle is highly metaphysical, a "new age" thinker. When the world doesn't keep up, stress results. *Note*: As with the other shapes, the squiggle under stress reveals his/her most **negative traits.** In the case of the squiggle, he/she will appear disorganized, impractical, unrealistic, illogical, uninhibited, evangelistic, eccentric and naive. More dramatic squiggles become very eccentric during stressful periods of life.

How to Identify a Squiggle Under Stress

1. Unanimated, listless movement around house/office
2. Boring to talk to; lacks usual enthusiasm
3. Loss of sense of humor

4. Emergence of unusual negative attitude
5. Critical of others (Squiggles are normally most critical of themselves.)
6. Severely disorganized and forgetful of commitments
7. Sloppy tendencies magnify into downright dirtiness
8. Can't hold the eye contact of another and mumbles
9. Wants to do wild and weird things never done before
10. Doesn't eat (squiggles have large appetites)
11. Not interested in sex
12. Watches TV (Squiggles are not TV watchers; there is not enough action!)
13. Asks advice of others (Although this is a healthy strategy for people under stress, it is abnormal for squiggles.)
14. Withdraws to be alone (This is when the squiggle retreats into that other reality. Although normal under favorable conditions, if very frequent, it's a danger signal.)

Sources of Stress for Squiggles

1. **Working in a Box Organization Alone Will Drive Squiggles Crazy!** As previously introduced, the worst situation for a squiggle is a *boring, routine job*, particularly one in which **quantity** of output is more important than the **quality** of the product.

2. **If the Squiggle Feels Undervalued at Work, This Is a Major Source of Stress.** The way the squiggle determines this is by the reactions of others to his/her ideas. If others routinely reject the ideas (squiggle's greatest gift), then he/she feels undervalued. *Note*: Since squiggles tend to "peak" early in life, later ideas may be of less value.

3. **Lack of Challenge in Life.** Squiggles seek new experiences daily. If there is no challenge at work, then they must find it elsewhere. If there is no challenge in their personal life either, they feel trapped and this is stressful.

4. **The Squiggle Is Often a Performer.** If there is no audience or an unappreciative audience, the squiggle is lost. *Note*: The squiggle vacillates between performer and recluse, in classic introvert fashion; for example, Michael Jackson.

Stressful People for Squiggles

1. **Boxes Are Number One on the Squiggle's "Hit" List!** The box and squiggle are like oil on water; they are literally opposite personalities. The box is the most left-brained, organized, practical, and inhibited of the shapes.

The squiggle is the most right-brained, creative, unrealistic, and flamboyant of the shapes. There will always be a natural conflict between these two shapes. If they are co-workers or married to one another, this is particularly difficult for both.

2. Triangles Cause Heartburn in Squiggles. The triangle wants to wield power and impose his/her ideas on the squiggle. The squiggle has ideas of his/her own. Unfortunately, the triangle is more often in the position of dominance over the squiggle.

Note: I have seen this relationship work well when the triangle is willing to listen to the ideas of the squiggle. The squiggle can produce more creative and unique ideas to help the company than the triangle can. If the triangle is willing to accept and implement the squiggle's ideas, everyone is happy. The squiggle produces the idea, and the triangle gets the credit!

Finally, the **circle** and **rectangle** are no problem for the squiggle. The circle is most capable of dealing with his/her eccentric behavior and the rectangle is a favorite because he/she is always willing to listen and learn new things.

How the Squiggle Deals with Stress

There are predictable *stages* that the squiggle will go through in dealing with a stressful period of life. Once you identify the development of these stages, you can assist your squiggle.

Stage 1: Recognition. This stage often takes some time to reach for the normally hectic stimulation-seeking squiggle. Since life is usually chaotic, the squiggle doesn't recognize that he/she is not coping well until some dramatic event occurs. This event can take the form of a spouse leaving the squiggle, a disciplinary session with the boss, or even the squiggle being fired from work.

Stage 2: Change of Situation. When the squiggle becomes aware of the stress, he/she first tries to solve the problem by changing the situation. He/she will run out and get another job/wife—whatever it takes to replace the original loss. Rarely does this solve the problem, because the squiggle will continue to make the same mistakes in the new job/relationship. He/she has not corrected the behaviors that caused the problem in the first place.

Stage 3: Stimulation-Seeking. When the change of situation doesn't work, the squiggle will regress into his/her most common mode of behavior: he/she will seek stimulation elsewhere. This is when the squiggle can get a little *weird*. Sources of stimulation for a squiggle are not your normal movie or dinner out. This is when the sky-diving or sudden trip to Hong Kong take place. Although they may provide a temporary relief from the squiggle's stress, the relief is not permanent. Once the new sources of stimulation get old, the stress is felt again.

Stage 4: Withdrawal. This is a natural outgrowth of the squiggle's tendencies. Squiggles are creatures of extremes. They are either very outgoing and dramatic, or they become very withdrawn and reclusive. Withdrawal is not a problem unless it is done in the extreme, with long periods of time in which the squiggle will not see or talk to anyone.

Stage 5: Depression. This is serious. If you know that your squiggle friend/mate is truly depressed, you must help him/her to seek professional services of a licensed counselor.

How to Help Your Squiggle to Reduce Stress

Before your squiggle reaches Stage 5, there are things that you can do to help reduce the stress that leads to this conclusion. If you are a major supportive person in your squiggle's life, you will need to know the following:

1. Try to Ensure an Adequate Balance of Excitement and Downtime in Your Squiggle's Life. Realize that the squiggle will require more excitement than the normal person, but he/she also needs some quiet time. The squiggle is normally a high-energy person, he/she must have time to revitalize that strong energy source.

2. Allow Your Squiggle to Be Alone Part of the Time. More than any of the other shapes, the squiggle needs time to be apart from others to "weave webs of great thought." You must accept this need and avoid smothering the squiggle by keeping people around all of the time.

3. Don't Put a Damper on the Squiggle's Ideas. Although some of them will be off-the-wall and totally unrealistic, they are the lifeblood of the squiggle.

4. Encourage the Squiggle's Use of His/Her Intuition. This is a natural talent within the squiggle. It is often discouraged or downplayed in this society. Encourage your squiggle to use it on his/her own behalf to prevent him/herself from getting into dangerous situations. The squiggle must learn to trust his/her "gut feelings," which are usually accurate.

5. Take Care of the Logistics. Squiggles are weak in matters of detail. They appreciate someone else doing this for them. It eliminates a source of stress.

6. Be a Realistic Sounding Board for Your Squiggle. Make sure that he/she trusts you enough to bring you his/her thoughts and problems. If so, you will be in a position to discourage any actions which you feel will be ultimately harmful to the squiggle.

7. Finally, Do Not Allow Total Withdrawal. This is a very dangerous tendency. Squiggles have been known to disappear for days without anyone

knowing their whereabouts. Keep close tabs on the daily movements of your squiggle, particularly if you know that he/she is already experiencing some stress.

Squiggles Feel Happiest When . . . .

1. They have just thought up a great **new idea!**
2. Others are **receptive** to their ideas.
3. They have a **new job.**
4. They are involved in a **new relationship.**
5. They have conquered a **difficult problem.**
6. They have just accepted a new **challenge.**
7. They are **recognized** by others as intelligent and/or creative.
8. There is a goodly amount of **excitement** in their lives.
9. There is enough time **alone** to think and revitalize themselves.
10. World leaders are concerned with the **future implications** of their actions.
11. Research into our **future in space** is taking place.
12. There is an adoring **audience** for the performance of our flamboyant and dramatic squiggle.

Section Six

SHAPE FLEXING

QUICK INDICATORS OF SHAPES

	BOX	TRIANGLE	RECTANGLE	CIRCLE	SQUIGGLE
Traits:	Organized Detailed Knowledgeable Analytical Determined Persevering Patient	Leader Focused Decisive Ambitious Competitive Bottom-line Athletic	In transition Exciting Searching Inquisitive Growing Courageous	Friendly Nurturing Persuasive Empathic Generous Stabilizing Reflective	Creative Conceptual Futuristic Intuitive Expressive Motivating Witty/Sexy
Common Words:	logistics deadlines allocate policy efficiency analysis I did it!	interface escalate jargon thrust ROI "expletives" You do it!	unsure consider maybe delegate options wait Why?	lovely gut-level comfort team cooperate feelings No problem!	experiment challenge create develop conceive begin What if?
Appearance—Men:	conservative short hair no facial hair	stylish appropriate expensive	erratic changeable facial hair	casual no tie youthful	sloppy dramatic dirty
Appearance—Women:	understated navy, grey, brown thin	tailored manicured briefcase	erratic extreme unusual	overweight feminine faddish	varied artistic fat/thin

BOX	TRIANGLE	RECTANGLE	CIRCLE	SQUIGGLE
		Office:		
every pencil in place	status symbols	mishmash	comfortable	messy
computer	awards	imitator	home-like	bleak or
	powerful	disorganized	plants	dramatic
		Body Language:		
stiff	composed	clumsy	relaxed	animated
controlled	jaunty	nervous	smiling	theatrical
poker face	piercing eyes	fleeting eyes	direct eyes	mercurial
nervous laugh	pursed mouth	giggle	full laugh	sexual cues
high-pitched voice	power voice	high-pitched voice	mellow voice	fast talk
twitches	mesomorph	silent	talkative	mannerisms
slow movement	smooth moves	jerky moves	head nods	fast moves
precise gesture	large gesture	flushed face	excessive touching	no touch
perspiration			attractive	high energy
		Personal Habits:		
loves routine	interrupts	forgetful	easy-going	spontaneous
put in writing	game player	nervous	joiner	disorganized
always prompt	early arriver	late or early	hobbies	rebellious
neat	joke teller	outbursts	sloppy	works alone
planner	power handshake	avoids	good cook	life of party
precise	fidgety	variety	patriotic	daydreams
collector	addictions	blurts out	TV watcher	interrupts
social loner	work/play hard	packrat	socializer	fickle

Chapter 22

Flexing on a TEAM

This section is divided into two important chapters: "Flexing with Finesse" and "Shape Evolution." Examine the Quick Indicator of Shapes found on pages 172 and 173. Now that you know which shape you are and the characteristics of your shape, it is important to understand that you are capable of "shape flexing."

Because all five shapes co-exist within each of us, we are blessed with the ability to **flex** from one shape to another as we adjust and adapt to the needs of others. We discussed the how-to's for dealing with bosses, spouses, and children of different shapes. When you communicate with others of different shapes, you are doing what I call *flexing* from your dominant shape to their dominant shape.

We are all capable of short-term flexing. This means that you can flex to another person's shape on a moment's notice. Some people do this purposefully. Others (like the circle) do it unconsciously. This chapter will explain the difference. Understanding the concept of flexing will assist you in improving your communication with others throughout your life!

Unconscious Flexing

1. **The Process.** Unconscious flexing is primarily an automatic human condition. When it is important for you to communicate successfully with someone else, you will automatically put yourself in the other person's shoes. In communication theory, this is called *receiver-orientation*. When we are receiver-oriented, we tend to be the best communicators.

2. **How It Works.** Simply put, when we think first of the other person (receiver)—not first of ourselves—is when we communicate best. We try

to think of how the other person will react and respond to what we have to say. **Example:** the boss is a triangle. He/she wants to hear the "bottom line" and is concerned about what's in it for him/her. If you are receiver-oriented, you will think like the boss and structure your message accordingly.

3. Thinking Versus Feeling. When we flex naturally, we do so with both the *cognitive* (intellectual) and the *affective* (emotional) parts of ourselves. Not only do we *think* like the other person thinks, but we also *feel* what he/she is feeling. This is called establishing **empathy.**

In unconscious flexing, this entire process happens automatically. You don't stop to think about it. You don't plan it that way, it just happens.

Conscious Flexing

The conscious flexing process is identical to the unconscious with one exception, it is not automatic. You, the communicator, are *aware* of speaking in the other person's language. You are purposefully choosing to flex to his/her shape. Prior to the communication event, the conscious flexor prepares him/herself in the following manner:

1. Analyze Your Target Person. What shape is he/she?

2. Consider the Characteristics of His/Her Shape. Think about both strengths and weaknesses. Use prior interactions with this person to **pinpoint** predictable behaviors.

3. Consider the Situational Context in Which Your Interaction Will Take Place. If others are to be present, how does this person react in a group? How will the specific personalities of the others affect your target person? How can you use them to your advantage?

4. Consider the Situational Content. How does your target person react on this particular subject? Although he/she may be one dominant shape in most situations, in certain cases, he/she may flex to another shape. You must be aware of this in order to receiver-orient your communication.

Conscious Flexing Scenario

Let's say that your target person is your boss. The purpose of your communication is to ask for a salary raise. You have made an appointment and your goal is to receive a 12 percent raise for the coming salary period. You *must* be successful, so you decide to use conscious flexing. Here are four steps for you to follow:

Step 1: You determine your boss's dominant shape. You decide, for example, that he/she is a circle.

Step 2: You carefully analyze the characteristics of people who are circles:

- They are social and need to be liked.
- They are concerned with other's opinions of their actions.
- They are equally interested in feelings and objective data.
- They have trouble making quick decisions. They need to check with others first.

Step 3: Consider the **situational context**. Since your boss has an "open door" policy, people often stop in to talk and interrupt appointments at will. You must arrange this meeting so that there will be no interruptions. You need the boss's full attention on this subject. Plus, you do not want your co-workers to be involved in this very private matter.

Solution: Take the boss to lunch before your 1 P.M. appointment. Circles love the social setting. This will give you the opportunity to establish the necessary rapport on a personal level before you make your request. Once back to the boss's office, casually close the office door to ensure privacy.

Step 4: Consider the **situational context**. Circles are particularly uncomfortable dealing with the realities of being **the boss**. Things like performance appraisals and salary reviews are very upsetting to them because they abhor the idea of having to choose between people and dislike giving negative feedback.

Solution: Let the circle's proclivity to please people work in your favor. Let the boss know that he/she will truly disappoint you if you do not receive this salary increase. Be prepared for the circle to argue from the point of **fairness** to your co-workers; that is, your increase would be unfair to those who will not receive one. Do not let this argument waylay you. Provide the necessary data to prove that you, indeed, do deserve this.

By following these four steps, you will increase the probability that your request will be granted. You will be practicing conscious flexing with your boss.

Flexing Hints for Each Shape

Each geometric shape is either left- or right-brain dominant. For this reason, each shape will react favorably to certain **appeals** based on hemispheric dominance. There are three classic appeals (à la Aristotle) which tend to convince certain types of people: (1) **logos** (logical appeal), (2) **ethos** (ethical appeal), and (3) **pathos** (emotional appeal). Once you know the correct appeal to use, you will be more successful in flexing to another person's shape. Below is a listing of which type of appeal works best with each shape.

1. Boxes: Logos. The box prefers **objective data** presented in a sequential fashion.

2. Triangles: Ethos. The triangle is the rule-maker, and life is a matter of right/wrong . . . . black/white.

3. Rectangles: Blend. Because the rectangle is the shape in transition, he/she can behave like any of the other four shapes at any time. Thus, all three appeals are possible choices, given the shape that the rectangle is flexing to at the moment.

4. Circles: Pathos. Circles are most easily swayed by an emotional appeal.

5. Squiggles: Ethos. Like the triangle, the black/white belief system comes into play for the squiggle. However, the squiggle's ethical appeal has a different intellectual underpinning than that of the triangle. Whereas the triangle is swayed by what is right based on logic (logos), the squiggle decides what is right based on the creative process. *Note*: Aristotle had no appeal for the right brain; he didn't know about brain theory yet.

Flexing "Hooks" for Each Shape

These are the *how-to's* in using the appeals I have previously mentioned. If you approach your shape in the correct manner, you will "hook" him/her to your point of view.

1. Box Hooks: Present your information with total objectivity and clarity . . . . in an almost "clinical" manner. Do not allow emotions or emotional language to cloud the issue. Put it in writing whenever possible. This makes it seem to be more objective.

2. Triangle Hooks: Present your proposal as the "only *right* way to do it!" Provide analysis but do not belabor the point. Get to the bottom line.

3. Rectangle Hooks: Good luck! This is the toughest one of all. You must first decide which shape the rectangle is flexing into at the moment. Then, choose the correct appeal for that shape. Be ready to change your appeal during the conversation for the mercurial rectangle.

4. Circle Hooks: Use lots of effect. You must let the circle know that this is **important to you,** that you would be disappointed if the circle did not grant your wish. Become upset if things don't go your way. Also, point out how others **feel** about it. If others support you, the circle will be more likely to do the same.

5. Squiggle Hooks: Get excited! The squiggle needs to see lots of enthusiasm and energy behind your proposal. Use words like **new, unique revolutionary idea.** Like hooking a triangle, show that you are convinced that your way is the right way.

Major Geometric Conflicts

There are certain shape combinations that signal built-in conflict with one another. By identifying these conflict combos, you will be better prepared to use your flexing hooks more effectively.

1. Box/Squiggle Conflict: The most organized has difficulty with the most disorganized. These two shapes are antithetical. They are the most opposite to one another.

Flexing: The box must learn to tolerate the random and spontaneous excitement of the squiggle. The box must learn to value the squiggle's creative ideas.

The squiggle must try to be more organized and logical when presenting information to the box. The squiggle should calm down a bit and try not to appear so emotional.

2. Triangle/Circle Conflict. The triangle is a fast mover and often treads over people on his/her tenacious climb upward. The circle finds the triangle to be self-centered and insensitive; the triangle dismisses the circle's concern.

Flexing: The triangle needs the circle to balance his/her dogmatism. In order to become a truly effective leader, the triangle must learn to take the needs of the people into consideration when making decisions.

The circle must exercise his/her ability to look past the outward roaring of the triangle, into the core of this very smart and confident person. When the circle learns to value the triangle for who he/she is, the circle will be one of his/her strongest supporters.

3. Box/Circle Conflict: The box is "all business" and circle is "all people." This is where the conflict lies. Also, the box tends to be the least in touch with his/her feelings, where the circle is constantly in touch with personal feelings and the feelings of others.

Flexing: The box must learn to give a little by sharing more of him/herself with the circle. Circles must know and trust their co-workers and colleagues.

The circle may need to develop a higher comfort level in working with someone who tends to be quiet and unrevealing.

4. Triangle/Squiggle Conflict: The triangles sees the squiggle as scattered and lacking appropriate seriousness. The squiggle thinks that the triangle is an egomaniac with no sense of humor. They come head-to-head when they disagree, and the battle can become violent. Both want it their way.

Flexing: The triangle can learn to talk ideas with the creative squiggle. The squiggle can learn to respect the decisive leadership of the triangle. The squiggle should use the technique of **implanting ideas** that the triangle will translate into action. (Of course, the squiggle must be prepared to receive no credit for his/her idea.)

Rectangle/Everyone Conflict: The rectangle is constantly changing and unpredictable for others. This makes him/her difficult to deal with.

Solution: Each of the other shapes can **flex** to the dominant style of the rectangle in given circumstances. Although this is difficult, it is also transitory. The rectangle will pass through this stage. We can only hope that the damage will be minimal for the rectangle during this period.

Triangle/Triangle Conflict: The only shape that has conflict within its own shape family is the dominant triangle. Two triangles together cause huge sparks to fly when they disagree. Both are accustomed to having others give in to them.

Flexing: Triangles who work/live together must establish an uneasy truce of sorts. They can flex to one another by agreeing to disagree within an atmosphere of **mutual respect.** They must learn to listen to one another and to respect the strength that both possess. If this is accomplished, two triangles can become close friends and colleagues.

Chapter 23

Shape Evolution

Just as we flex shapes to adjust to difficult people and situations on a daily basis, we also flex naturally throughout life. As we mature and our bodies and minds age, we begin to see life differently. As we grow older, the things that once seemed *so* important, no longer seem so vital. Another way of describing this change in perspective is **shape evolution**.

There are some predictable **life stages** that occur for many Americans. These have been identified in recent years by sociologists and psychologists (Erickson, Piaget, Massey, et al.). In the beginning of this chapter, we will look at these life stages through the prism of Psycho-Geometrics.

In the final section of this chapter, I will describe the natural evolutionary process for each shape. This is a positive and hopeful section, because if you don't like certain aspects of your shape, you can and will change them. This natural movement to a more positive state comes with age.

THE LIFE STAGES

The Pre-School Squiggles

This is a life stage of unabashed creativity and spontaneity. The young child has just entered this big, beautiful world. There is so much to explore and to learn. The attention span is short, the excitement overflowing. Actions and reactions are primarily **intuitive** and **natural**. Although the parent must apply certain controls, the linear brain programming is not complete and the most genuine, spontaneous qualities of the right brain are evident.

The "Star Student" Box

The minute this creative spirit is socked into the American school system, a necessary flexing must occur *if* he/she is to be a successful student. The random, unmonitored behaviors of the squiggle must be controlled—the linear, logical systems are activated. The **box** emerges. Some children flex easily to this new life requirement, others have difficulty subverting their natural squiggle and implanting their box.

Adolescent Confusion

Enter the **rectangle**. What is the world really about? Who am I? What am I to become? Who should be my friends? Who should be my hero? Why are these crazy parents making me do these awful things? What is this terrible world that I find myself in?

All of this is painful for the teenager, and equally as painful for the "stupid" parents who experience it. The box has flexed into a rectangle. This is a transitional stage which is necessary as the person progresses to adulthood.

Young Married Bliss

Ah . . . . how wonderful to be a **circle**! The age 20 to 29 period seems to define a new flexing: the rectangle fades, and the circle replaces it. People in young adulthood tend to define themselves through others: friends, mates, spouses, bosses, etc. This is a time when most young couples have their first baby. All the warmth and nurturing of the circle emerges during this period.

The BOOM Period

Climbing the ladder, getting ahead, nose to the grindstone—all to establish oneself in a career. This is the hallmark of the **triangular thirties**. Sociologists call this the BOOM period (**B**ecoming **O**ne's **O**wn **M**an). (The concept must have been developed before women were working!) During this period, it is the **career** that is most important. It is often the time that people first become the BOSS. The circle subsides, and the roar of the triangle is heard!

The Mid-Life Crisis

Whoops . . . . here comes that **rectangle** again! Who am I? What is life really about? Why am I working 60 hours a week? What are my children really like? Who is this man/woman I live with? Isn't there more to life than this rat race I'm in?

This is a highly publicized time in life for Americans. Examples abound of people in their mid-forties who suddenly leave their good jobs, get divorced, and pursue a radical life style change. Although the emergence of the **rectangle** may trigger this life stage, the person may actually flex to the **squiggle** during the "acting out" period.

The Mellow Years

As Americans enter their late fifties and sixties, many testify that those things that were so important in earlier years just don't bother them anymore. What becomes important now is enjoying people and events which the remainder of this life has to offer. These are the "golden years" in which *harmony* with one's self and others is an attainable goal. For many, it is a time when the **circle** re-emerges.

For others, it is a time for their natural shape to **evolve** to a higher plane. Each shape has the capacity to evolve. The next section will describe the natural evolutions germane to each individual shape.

THE EVOLVED SHAPES

People can and do change. Sometimes it is the outer world that provokes the change. Other times we listen to our inner stirrings and follow the road not taken. This section is devoted to a description of each shape in its *evolved* state.

The Evolved Box

As the years pass, the box often finds him/herself in a rut of his/her own making. Whether he/she is able to break out of this rut will determine whether or not the box can evolve. It should be noted that many boxes live and die in the maze of self-imposed ritual and routine.

If the dissatisfaction grows strong enough, the box may evolve in one of two directions. The first and most likely evolution involves an assimilation of *triangle traits*. The box as follower now emerges as a triangular leader. Remember, the box always possessed the knowledge, he/she merely lacked the focus and courage to act on it.

The evolved box transcends this character flaw and develops the inner strength to be decisive. If this box person also develops the ability to communicate his/her decisions, then the evolved box is in a fine position to move from a position of responsibility to one of authority.

The personal life of the box is a different matter. A second evolution toward more *circular traits* is possible within the box. However, this can be excruciatingly painful for the unemotional, uninvolved box. This growth on the personal level is often triggered by an *external event*: divorce, loss or removal of a loved one. Suddenly, the stoic box becomes aware of his/her need for human intimacy. This newly discovered dependence can be shattering. Deeply embedded emotions may surface and threaten to drown the inexperienced box.

Although painful, this is a *necessary step* in the box's evolution to becoming a more sensitive, affectionate, feeling human being. If the transformation is complete, the result is wonderful. After years of closing him/herself off from others, the box welcomes loved ones with open arms and happy tears. The reservoir of emotion is released, and the warm waves gently melt the iceberg. Loved ones who are thirsty for this affection are instantly satiated. The box has evolved, the rough angles have been smoothed.

The Evolved Triangle

Particularly in the later years, many triangles relax and learn to enjoy life more fully. It is often not until this period that the strong triangle is able to sit back and enjoy the adoration of others. The younger "driver" allows someone else to take the wheel. He/she becomes interested in people and learns to trust others.

As a spouse, the **circle** emerges and enjoyment of the family peaks. Unfortunately, children are now grown and the grandchildren often reap the benefit of the triangle's evolution. Since the triangle is the prime candidate for mid-life crisis, this shift may be dramatic. The focus on career changes to a search for inner peace and loving companions. This is a time of dangerous pressure on a marriage.

As a parent, some triangles first become acquainted with their children in mid-life. If the circle surfaces strong, the triangle can do an about face, becoming uncharacteristically generous and truly loving. The evolved triangle finds joy in mere conversation (as long as partners adore him/her) and is capable of making peace with him/herself.

As a boss, the triangle can soften into a "benevolent dictator" in later career stages. Prone to demonstrate the "generative period" through mentoring, the triangle will show a proclivity toward favoritism.

Some triangles become excellent *leaders* in their late 50s, 60s, and early 70s. Their leadership style shifts from a self-centered, ambitious autocracy to a more democratic and paternal style. (It is impossible for a triangle to ever be a laissez-faire leader!) Scarred from many wars, the triangle is less likely to compete and confront; he/she is not so determined to win the battle. More willing to delegate, to listen, and to be open to the ideas of others, the triangle becomes a more effective leader.

Status becomes less important (often because the triangle already has it). This is an excellent time for the evolved triangle to engage in civic and social service. For some, the political arena is a natural progression. The mellowed, wiser triangle is an excellent candidate for political office because the natural leadership skills can now be used for the right reasons and not for self-aggrandizement.

Overall, the evolved triangle is a desirable leader who is capable of making major contributions to society. He/she is also (for the first time) a desirable partner.

Note: There is no "evolved rectangle." Rectangles are in a natural state of evolution and transition.

The Evolved Circle

In one sense, the evolution of the circle is unpleasant. Those who have come to depend upon this amiable, supportive, nurturing person are often dismayed and even actively angry over the change in the circle. However, those who truly return the love of their circle will understand and even applaud this metamorphosis.

Of all the shapes, the circle's evolution is the most painfully dramatic. The strongest circular trait—the need for people—lessens during the evolution. (Strangely, this is the very trait to which the boxes and triangles evolve!)

Circles are best known for their need to please others—to defer to others—to accommodate the needs of others. The evolution of the circle involves a hardening of this giving spirit. The circle in evolution moves away from pleasing others to pleasing self!

This change is often provoked by the circle's increasing resentment toward those who take advantage of his/her kind heart. As the years pass, the circle eventually tires of stepping aside to let others go first. He/she reaches a point of high-pitched anger toward a world that demands his/her social skills but refuses to accept the circle as a leader.

This realization often becomes most clear to circles who are thrust into a position of leadership. Over the years, they learn that, indeed, you can't please all of the people all of the time. When they attempt to do so, they suffer from the natural resentment of their subordinates who want the circle to take a stand, even if it's an unpopular one. When the circle does not, an insidious loss of respect develops that the circle boss must eventually come to grips with.

It is often at this point that the circular metamorphosis will occur. There are three stages in this evolution that simulate the traits of three other shapes; Stage 1—Squiggle, Stage 2—Box, and Stage 3—Triangle.

Stage 1: The most common first step is for the circle to assume **squiggle** traits, since both shapes are right-brain dominant. When the circle discovers that loving and caring for employees only goes so far when they disagree, the circle may become highly *creative* in finding solutions to problems. Because he/she is an excellent communicator, the circle may adopt the squiggle's dramatic, evangelistic techniques in presenting these solutions. He/she hopes to sell a workable compromise to both sides. This approach may work for awhile, but is rarely long-lasting.

Stage 2: When the circle discovers that his/her creative attempts at problem-solving aren't working, he/she will retreat and take on **box** characteristics. Refusing to openly deal with employees and feeling the need to do further research to defend his/her decisions, the circle will slip into the cold, aloof, removed posture of the box leader.

Of all the stages, this is the most difficult one for the circle's friends to deal with. This is an abrupt change in the affable circle personality. However, this is an important stage, for when the circle goes "underground," he/she discovers his/her true inner strength. The circle emerges with less dependence upon others and a sense of self-confidence that was often missing in the past.

Stage 3: When the circle emerges from the box stage, the change is much more desirable. Although the circle is still a circle (and always has been), there is a strengthening, a new courage. The circle has found within him/herself an inner strength and wisdom to face problems with both sensitivity and rationality. He/she has shed the need to make the popular decision and replaced it with the wisdom to seek and the courage to make the correct decision.

When the transition is complete, the evolved circle is the best choice for leadership of the four shapes! He/she carries the (1) genuine concern for people, (2) wisdom to see the "grays" of a problem, (3) creativity to forge a workable compromise, (4) knowledge of the job, (5) courage to make the tough decision, and (6) ability to communicate and to motivate the people in their best interests. The evolved circle is my choice for President!

Please note: This is a rather idealized scenario. In truth, few circles do evolve to this point. They may enter the prescribed stages but often get stuck in Stage 1 or 2; or they may finally retreat back to the familiar comfort of warm, fuzzy circlehood.

The Evolved Squiggle

It is only fair to tell you that an evolved squiggle is highly unlikely. *Once a squiggle, always a squiggle!* It is very difficult for this tiger to change his/her stripes. The squiggle is not only a personality type, it is a strong way of thinking and perceiving life. Oh, yes, the squiggle may experience a temporary evolution from time to time. But, don't be fooled, the creative bent and dramatic expression will re-emerge.

The temporary evolutions allow the squiggle to adapt to his/her life circumstances: (1) to do a box job from 8 to 5, (2) to behave as a loving circle when he/she needs an audience, and (3) to make a triangular argument in defense of a new idea. However, it is almost impossible for a squiggle to evolve to another shape.

The pure squiggle has a wanderlust; an unquenchable need to experiment, to explore, to discover. The need to withdraw into deep thought is juxtaposed to the equally strong need within the squiggle to emerge as the life of the party! Although these tendencies can be modified, they cannot be nullified.

In later years, some of the squiggle's indefatigable energy may wane. As the body ages, the ability to flit from person to person and country to country may cease. Along with the strokes and emphysema (squiggles do not give up smoking), come the blurred speech and belabored breath. But, if you look closely—if you peer deeply into the recesses of that hollow face—you will see those old eyes twinkle and sparkle with the undying spirit of our capricious squiggle.

SUMMARY

Psycho-Geometrics is a new **tool** for you to use in your life from this point onward. It will change the way you perceive and communicate with others. You have a new **gift** . . . . the gift of flexing from one shape within you to another. Use it when and how you can to improve relationships.

You have been given yet another gift . . . . the gift of fuller understanding of yourself and the changes that you experience within from time to time. Use these gifts wisely . . . . to benefit yourself and to benefit those whom you value in this life.

Just remember to . . . .

"Box your Boss!"
"Circle your Peers!"
"Triangle your Subordinates!"
and . . . . **"Squiggle your Lover!"**

SOME STEREOTYPIC SHAPE "COMBOS"

Charismatic Leader

Secretary

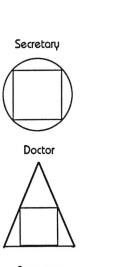

Supervisor

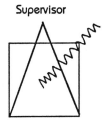

Salesperson

Doctor

Nurse

Attorney

Reporter

Teacher

Principal

Computer Programmer

A-I Specialist

Entrepreneur

Entry-Level Employee

5 Years Later

15 Years Later

187

The Theoretical Underpinnings of Psycho-Geometrics

Although Psycho-Geometrics is the "newest" of the personality theories available today, there is some very *old thinking behind it*. It is a blend of several disciplines of thought: psychology, sociology, anthropology, philosophy, architecture, theology, and astrology.

Historical Connections provides you with a quick reference chart. This chart illustrates ten dominant bodies of thought that have influenced our perception of human behavior over the last several hundred years. For purposes of clearer understanding, I have taken some liberties in grouping whole bodies of theory into four concise categories called "Four Aspects of Human Behavior." Academic integrity is maintained in the sense that most theories that attempt to define *human difference* do delineate four major aspects.

HISTORICAL CONNECTIONS

Four Aspects of Human Personality

	Analytic	Dominant	Social	Creative
Geometry	Square	Triangle	Circle	Squiggle
Ancient	Air	Earth	Water	Fire
Alchemy	Phlegmatic	Choleric	Melancholic	Sanguine
Medical	Type B	Type A	Type B	Type A
Brain Dominance	Left	Left	Both	Right
Anthropology	Ectomorph	Mesomorph	Endomorph	Ectomorph
Androgyny	Male	Male	Female	Female
Astrology	Virgo Taurus Capricorn	Aries Scorpio Leo	Cancer Libra Sagittarius	Aquarius Gemini Pisces
Art Theory	Blue	White/Black	Red	Yellow
Leadership Style	Autocrat	Democrat	Participative	Laissez-Faire
Management Style	Analytic	Director	Amiable	Expressive
Psychology	Realist	Pessimist	Optimist	Idealist
(Freud)	Superego	Superego	Id	Id
(Jung)	Thinker	Sensor	Feeler	Intuitor
(behavioral)	Introvert	Extrovert	Extrovert	Introvert
Religion				
Christian	cross	trinity	halo/rosary	serpent
Jewish	tau	star	tehom	caduceus
Hindu	yantra	pentacle	mandala	om
Buddhist	tori	ushnisha	aureole	lotus
Muslim	mosque	obelisk	golden cup	minaret
Egyptian	cartuche	pyramid	ankh	water
Greco-Roman	swastika	trident	omphalos	spiral
Celtic	calendar	mithras	stone circle	labyrinth

Epilogue (Circa 1998)

An International
_____Perspective

Before this new edition goes to press, I want to add this short section on "Communicating Beyond Our Differences In Foreign Lands." I have had the privilege of presenting my **Psycho-Geometrics**^{tm} System in 15 foreign nations as diverse as China, Ukraine, Australia, United Kingdom and most of Europe. The first edition of this book has been translated into Dutch and Russian. I have spoken to over one-half million people from every conceivable walk of life and I know the value of understanding human difference beyond the Atlantic and Pacific borders of the U.S. and Canada.

For centuries, humans have attempted to communicate. From the oldest cave drawings in France to the ancient stone carvings in Newgrange (north of Dublin), anthropologists have examined early methods of communication via crude ifactse Many drawings take the form of _symbols_ such as spirals, squares, and triangles. By applying the interpretations of the shapes to these symbols, we can learn more about the "cultural personality" of a country or people.

Many of my readers are now working in the global arena and have need of new, intercultural communication skills. The application of **Psycho-Geometrics**^{tm} in a foreign country is a great aid to salespeople, government liaisons, corporate managers, expatriots, and certainly to the world tourist.

Whether you are on your way for a 2-year overseas stint for your company or agency — or — you are merely planning a cruise to Australia, New Zealand and Southeast Asia; you will find this explication of symbols as they describe different cultures to be of value.

THE UNITED KINGDOM: A MIXED BAG OF SHAPES

Since most Americans seem to derive at least a portion of their ancestral heritage from the British Isles, it seems appropriate to begin with the U.K. Interestingly, there is a marked difference between the English, Scots and Irish when we apply the **Psycho-Geometrics**[tm] method of analysis.

I have presented my system in seminar settings in all three (3) regions over a period of ten (10) years. My sampling includes: 3,000 English, 500 Scots and 300 Irish. The cities range from large (London, Belgast, Edinburgh) to smaller ones (Nottingham, Aberdeen and Shannon).

The data hold true both within each region and as a generally shared perception of that region from the outside.

The English Box

There is a "right way and a wrong way" and we do it the right way in England! The English seem to typify our concept of the box personality. There are standards to be upheld within every arena of human life. Rules are of utmost importance and woe to the fellow who breaks an English law! From Parliament to Buckingham Palace traditions are sacred.

The following is a short list of English characteristics and behaviors which qualify this culture as a "box personality;"

1.   Value of tradition, i.e. Monarchy
2.   High standards: personal & professional
3.   Inviolate justice system
4.   Emphasis on proper manners; rules of etiquette
5.   Adherence to hierarchical organization structures
6.   Absolute class system; inherited social status
7.   Equitable application of rule systems
8.   Colonization of the "English Right Way" i.e. India
9.   Conservative political position
10. Fierce defense of country/family
11. Perfectionistic tendency as demonstrated in academic scholarship, global negotiations, and work ethic
12. Personal rigidity in social interactions

Tips for communicating with English

Nonverbal:

1. Proxemics: allow sufficient "personal space" when interacting (3-4 feet is comfortable distance between people in polite conversation as compared to $1^1/_2$–2 feet in the U.S.)
2. Establish and maintain direct eye contact at all times (Americans use more casual eye contact)
3. Body posture should be erect and slightly stiff
4. Remain standing — do not sit unless invited (sitting indicates a much longer interaction)
5. Control excess gesticulation: be calm and controlled using a minimum of gesture & facial expression
6. Practice your handshake — theirs is excellent!
7. Dress professionally: understatement with quality (nothing flamboyant)
8. Neat and clean are requisite!

Verbal:

1. Speak ENGLISH! i.e. proper grammar please
2. Eliminate regional dialects ("y'all come" or "warsh your clothes" doesn't cut it!)
3. Get a travel guidebook and learn English terms i.e. venue for hotel, pub for bar, etc.
4. Do not use swear words. If you must, use "bloody" (roughly translated to mean shitty)
5. Avoid *personal questions*; i.e. Where do you live? What do you do for a living?
6. Be succinct when you speak & do not interrupt
7. Apply good manners at all times!
8. Learn to "listen first, talk last" & *slow down*

Remember history: The English DO like Americans — we came to their aid in World War II and they haven't forgotten it. They allow us our eccentricities and often think of us as childlike; "Just another crazy American, you know." But . . . if you will follow the guidelines above, you will elicit more respect from an English Box.

Note: The guidelines suggested above are equally applicable in the country of *New Zealand*. Zealanders are English expats who should not be confused with Australian squiggles.

The Scottish Triangle

The Scots are a different story. Perhaps it's the Celtic blood, who knows? There's a determined streak that smacks of our triangle. Whereas the English can be more forgiving, you mustn't ever cross a Scot. And a Scotsman is NOT an Englishman!

Although some of the characteristics above do apply, some of the marked differences are as follows:

1. Speed up the pace of your speech
2. Don't shout even when they do
3. Get ready to look up to establish eye contact (average height is 6'2" for men)
4. Take money — YOU will buy the ale!
5. Don't be intimidated — reread triangle chapters
6. Have a joke ready — they love it!
7. You can ask more personal questions; they will
8. Swearing is permitted (in pubs)
9. Tea time is still sacred
10. Avoid discussing politics or religion (unless you're Presbyterian)

Note: The Scots are great negotiators (like most triangles). (Remember who created Hong Kong!) Be prepared!

Irish Squiggles

Ah, the Irish! Unlike the plunging waterfall of the Scottish triangles, here the Celtic blood flows as a bubbling brook bouncing gaily down the hillside. But, beware — that same Irish brook can suddenly overflow its boundaries and become a raging flood of emotion! After several pints of Guinness, the pink-skinned Irish can flush beet-red in the face and turn pugilistic in a flash.

But the Irish are truly the "squiggles" of the British empire (both Ireland proper and Northern Ireland). They *love* to have fun and the young workers do fill the pubs. In many ways, they feel more aligned with Americans than with either the Scots or the English. They are wonderful hosts and do know that their bread is buttered by American tourism. They want to spend time with you and will talk and talk and talk. . . .

Some tips in communicating with Irish Squiggles:

1. They will buy the ale for you!
2. In return you are expected to sit and listen
3. You can be as demonstrative as you like (they think the English are bores)
4. Do enjoy the childlike quality: honesty is vital (they will tell you anything)
5. Do your business first (while sober); don't mix business & pleasure
6. Personal questions are okay, but don't push
7. Avoid politics and religion
8. Be a bit flamboyant, but don't outdo your host
9. Pick up pace of speech, don't stare, use hearty laugh, and relax and enjoy it!

Note: In a business setting, avoid tendency to take advantage of the Irish squiggles. Around the edges of this culture you may see the eyes of the British "stepchild" peeking out. While they are friendly and fiercely independent, the waves of history surround their shores.

German Triangle/Boxes

The second most prevalent ancestral heritage in the U.S. is the German. My experience in presenting seminars and traveling in this nation points directly to the *linear personality* as we have defined it in **Psycho-Geometrics.**[tm]

It seems unfair to group all Germans into the triangle type, for they are not all dogmatic, dominant, and egocentric. Munich is not Hamburg. Berlin is not Cologne. However, the Germans DO carry a definite strength and determination which interlaces their everyday living and interactions. This triangular strength can be very enviable when it is focused toward a positive end.

The German personality is similar to the English as both coalesce around the Box. Germans too have definite rule systems — both personally and professionally. There is a "right way." Both cultures share some basic values:

1. Strong work ethic
2. Practicality first in all decisions
3. Personal hygiene
4. Close family commitment
5. Daily planning & routines
6. Organized patterns of living
7. Personal discipline

However, it is difficult to ignore that special German PRIDE that is most identified with our triangle. There is that deep river that runs underneath the surface of what Nietzsche called the "Will to Power".

My family name was Roush (a.k.a. Rausch = "red & drunken"). Anyone who has grown up in a family with strong German roots must know the impact of the German triangle/box. The box believes in the rules and the triangle is glad to write them.

Tips for communicating with German Triangle/Boxes

Nonverbal:

1. The same erect body posture of the English
2. More gesticulation — LARGE, sweeping gestures
3. Very direct eye contact
4. Preference for standing to do business
5. May use personal space invasion if combative (moving within 12" of partner)
6. Powerful handshake with excessive arm shaking (be ready)
7. Facial expression often sullen or pokerface — smiling reserved for family gatherings and the Octoberfest libations
8. May use pointing gestures to emphasize (do not allow to intimidate)

Verbal:

1. Focused and clipped speech (enhanced by German language plosives)
2. Faster pacing in conversation (about 300 wpm compared to American 250)
3. Direct communication — Germans get to the point! (no hesitation)

4.   Minimal use of descriptive words — succinct message conveyance
5.   Typically employ low pitch voice property — can significantly increase voice volume when drinking
6.   Singing is universal language (brush up on your Wagner opera)

Note: Although not to the same degree as the Brits, the Germans are also class conscious and also somewhat prejudiced against ~~other~~ blacks and women (in my experience). If you fall into one of those categories, using strong and focused verbal and nonverbal communication will elicit respect from the German triangle. Strength respects strength.

Russian Triangle/Circles

Of all the people in the world, I find the Russians and Ukrainians to be closest to the Germans. However, they are definitely Bavarian German. This means that the outer manifestation of self is that of a triangle, but the inner core is definitely circular! They are truly a warm and loving people at heart and do expect lots of tactile communication in the form of a massive BEAR HUG!

Note: Do include the Finnish culture in this analysis. The same tips that work with Russians apply to the Finns also.

Tips on communicating with Russians

Nonverbal:

1.   Just "read the face" — it's all there. Until a Russian trusts you, he/she will maintain a triangle's glower. Once you are accepted, the face of a mercurial circle appears.
2.   Smile warmly — present your circle first
3.   Be demonstrative — Russians warm to flamboyant gestures and body language
4.   Laugh alot! Russians have a highly developed sense of humor (Finns too). Use a belly laugh.
5.   Use excessive touching: enclose Russian hand in both of yours for handshake, hug often, and don't be embarrassed when men walk down the street arm in arm.

Verbal:

1. Use of English is not yet so good — be patient as they struggle
2. Pace quickens as they get excited (which is often) (can escalate to 350–400 wpm)
3. Voice pitch is low as with Germanic counterparts
4. Because of language difficulties, Russians will often interpret our message by reading nonverbal gestures, facial expression and voice tone (be sure these are congruent with your message)
5. Like the Irish, Russians can become combative quickly — be sure to apologize first if this occurs. Then, soften situation with humor and you are forgiven.
6. As before, best to avoid politics and religion (many commoners despise Yeltsin & Gorbachev)

Cultural Tips:

Point 1: Drinking is akin to a sacred ritual here.
If you can't drink warm Vodka, don't go! There are no mixers in most Russian homes so your best bet is a flavored vodka (pepper is not bad). Socializing means drinking.

Point 2: Women seem to receive more respect here and gender differences are slight. Racial diversity is nonexistent.

Point 3: Don't ever compliment someone's jewelry or belongings. The culture requires the Russian to return the compliment by immediately giving it to you as a gift!

Southeast Asian Box/Rectangle

Swiftly we move to the far southeastern corner of the Asian continent where everyday is "business as usual." I refer directly to Hong Kong, Singapore and the emerging city-states of Kuala Lumpur, Malaysia and Jakarta, Indonesia. Many Americans and Europeans are now doing business in these emerging cultures.

Although there are differences, the *overseas Chinese* hold the wealth and are in control. (*Fortune Magazine*, 1/96). Thus, any analysis of the shape personalities of southeast Asia must inevitably lead to an analysis of the Chinese. The Chinese culture is multi-faceted, but tradition looms large and carries with it the strong Box personality. However, there is CHANGE in the air — from Hong Kong to Kuala Lumpur. *This region elected a Rectangle to describe itself in 4/96.*

Cultural Values:

1. The first commitment is always to the Chinese nation (by both mainland and overseas Chinese)
2. Family comes second — extended family is prevalent
3. Because this culture is steeped in history and tradition, the rules of living are absolute (no squiggles)
4. Religious values play a large part in everyday life with Buddha's path leading the way (Indonesians and Malaysians have more tolerance and some follow Krishna, Christ, or Mohammed)
5. Although Western ways and ideology are "creeping in" to the lifestyles of the young, the old traditions still dominate
6. The elderly are revered and sought out for their wisdom (unlike our culture)
7. Leadership is absolute and decisions are made to balance the good of the whole with the need to maintain control by the leaders
8. Hong Kong is the Chinese "experiment" in doing business with the West. However, Singapore has now eclipsed Hong Kong as the center of business for the overseas Chinese. *Singapore is classic BOX culture.*
9. Malaysia and Indonesia are emerging countries, they are RECTANGULAR now, but are only pausing within this shape momentarily. During this time they are unpredictable and *need respect and validation.*

Tips for communicating with Chinese

Nonverbal:

1. Think British . . . demonstrating personal control is important — no flamboyance
2. Showing respect is critical (bowing is common — be sure to give the last bow)
3. Use little gesture — arms held against the torso is typical
4. Offering the Western handshake is acceptable when doing business — bowing best in the home
5. Exercise cautious eye contact — do not stare! Do look down often and avert eyes

6. Sit instead of standing — this equalizes height differential and shows respect

7. Learn to drink saki and eat raw foods and — most importantly — to use chopsticks

8. Making noises when eating (i.e. slurping soup) is considered good manners

9. Do not wear street shoes in Chinese home and *always* bring a small gift (nothing elaborate)

10. When in Singapore, follow all rules of the citystate without question (there are many)

11. Be clean without heavily perfumed body scent (women — wear minimal make-up)

Verbal:

1. Speak in hushed tones — with soft volume and slightly higher pitch level

2. Practice disciplined listening and never interrupt

3. Slow pace of speech (approximately 200 wpm)

4. When gesturing, make slow and specific gestures to indicate direction (knot emotion)

5. Reflect mood of host — be jovial if appropriate, but never crass or loud. Do not get drunk even if host does.

6. Speak positively about city, home decor, and Eastern lifestyle (praise symbols of success)

7. Avoid any semblance of belief that Western ways are superior

8. Prepare to lose negotiation on price of products or services. Southeast Asians KNOW the value of their products and do not need to negotiate. If this is necessary, hire a Chinese intermediary.

Note: It is important to note that Hong Kong is much more "westernized" than the other countries mentioned. However, they do not respond favorably to being pressured. It is best not to leave a bad impression. The extended family "network" can destroy reputations. Remember 2,000 — Century of the Dragon!

Australian Squiggles

As many have said, Australia is like America twenty years ago. So true. Although there are some marked differences, there are also striking similarities with the America of the 1970's.

Cultural values/behaviors:

1. Live now — tomorrow will take care of itself!
2. Work is just a way to make the money needed to play
3. Family values are important, but individual values take precedence
4. Government is a necessary evil to take care of us
5. Don't get uptight — laid back is cool
6. Stay out of world affairs — maybe they'll forget we're down here
7. Politics and religion are personal basically boring anyway
8. We can't wait to save enough money to visit the U.S.!
9. We like American movies (love that Mel Gibson), but still have enough British to enjoy opera & theatre
10. Play, play, play . . . one life to live!

Tips for communicating with Aussie Squiggles

Nonverbal/Verbal:

1. *Casual always* — no ties or constricting clothing - the gauzy flowing garments of the American '70's flower children are in style
2. Soft behaviors and gestures — accent friendliness
3. Relaxed speech patterns. Slow down and don't push.
4. Allow plenty of time – don't rush. Aussies will make up their own minds
5. Be American . . . they love us. Be sure to include the socializing period. Break a few rules to identify with the squiggles, but don't overdo the outrageous! Remember—they ARE British by heritage.

Note: I could have as easily typified the Aussies as Circle/ Boxes — but by their own preference — they think of themselves as Squiggles. A warning: remember their British heritage and realize that, if they sense you are ingenuine, they can revert to the British Box quickly.

The Mediterranean Circles

Here we have a true "Circle Culture". As much as the twist! Italians, Spanish & Greek feel they are totally different from one another, they all share the Circle personality. You can throw in southern France, but you must add the more complex elements of the triangular elitism and the definite proclivities of the squiggle as well. These Mediterranean countries seem to share the following definitive values:

Cultural values:

1. Family is all.
2. Culture (as it is defined by lifestyle) is next.
3. The lifestyle is always personable, friendly, playful, and even loving — yet steeped in the knowledge that their time (as global leaders) is passed
4. Tradition is strong and is centered in religion
5. The Spanish "siesta" is practiced throughout this area — defining lifestyle of pleasure, not business
6. Personal and work life is much more casual and relaxed than the northern European
7. Personal accomplishment and discipline are much less valued and stressed than in other European countries and England
8. Personal relationships (friends of both genders) are of paramount importance — even though they are often recognized as temporary liaisons
9. Forget meticulous personal habits, etiquette, and hygiene — let's get on with the living instead!

Tips in communicating with Mediterraneans

Nonverbal:
1. Large, relaxed gestures
2. Open and genuine feelings expressed via facial expressions and language
3. Casual clothing, but fashionable and high quality
4. Voice patterns reflecting fluid expression of thought and feeling
5. Sitting and socializing most common interactive pattern

Verbal:

1.   Discuss personal concerns and situations
2.   Express feelings often — often with dramatic flair and emot
3.   Acknowledge tradition and history and take great pride i accomplishments of the past (give some credit to Spain i improved economic status in the latter part of this century)
4.   Use slower speech patterns and lower pitch level
5.   Laughter is valued and encouraged in all situations

The Japanese Box/Circles

For full explication of the "box personality" of the Japanese people, r refer to the section on Southeast Asians — the same principles apply. ever, it is important to note that the"circle" portion of the Japanese cul used to define their decision-making processes. In Japan, decisions a made by individuals, but by groups called "kieretsus." These are *policy-n teams that function much like the enclosed circle of a family.* This is : frustrating experience for American business people, because final dec must be made by the team — not a singular leader.

America: The Melting Pot

One of the joys of living in this nation is the benefit of the blending of the r cultures and nationalities that have been described in the preceding pag this Epilogue. As much as we think of ourselves as a "melting pot," it mus recognized that other nations perceive a distinct and definable Amer culture that is described in one word: *Squiggle!*

Remember a basic principle in **Psycho-Geometrics;**^{tm} *regardless how; perceive yourself, it is of value to understand how others perceive you.*

If we are perceived as squiggles, then this is the behavior that is expec of us when we travel to other nations. We can both improve our relationsh and surprise our hosts by "flexing" to the customs and personalities of th nation rather than our own. These final pages assist you in understand how to apply the personality analysis of **Psycho-Geometrics**^{tm} to cultu other than our own.

Symbols of Nations

Can you find the characteristic "shape personality" in each country's symbol?...

(Source: *Signs of Life* by Angela Arrienes)

GERMANY

SPAIN

SCOTLAND

AFRICA

JAPAN

MEXICO

IRELAND

INDIA